THE GOOD THIEF:
A Mystery of Mercy

Fr. André Daigneault

Originally published in French

Anne Sigier Editions
1073, boul. René-Lévesque Ouest

The Good Thief
by André Daigneault

ECUMENICAL ENGLISH edition
Published by Prison Fellowship International www.pfi.org
Under license from © Éditions Anne Sigier
Website: www.annesigier.qc.ca

Printed in the United States of America

ISBN 1-59781-358-3

All Scripture quotations are from the *New Revised Standard Version,* American edition, © 1989 by Oxford University Press.

Cover: Statue of the Good Thief by Michel Laude and displayed at Notre-Dame de Bercy (Paris)
Photo: Pierre François

www.xulonpress.com

CONTENTS

DEDICATION

To Mister Yves Carrer, a lay apostle who, for more than thirty years, has been laboring to make the holy Good Thief known and loved. Without his support, and encouragement and his collaboration as well as the documentation he has given me, this book would not have been published.

Preface

"Like the Good Thief I want to appear before Him
with empty hands."
Thérèse of Lisieux

Eighteen years before I was ordained as a priest, I wrote:

> Lord, if, someday, you make me a priest, I would
> like to be the priest of your heart and your mercy.
> Mercy, forgiveness, love for sinners, spiritual child-
> likeness, and in unity with my friends in heaven:
> Thérèse of Lisieux, the holy Curé of Ars (St. Jean-
> Marie Baptiste Vianney), St. Louis-Marie Grignion
> de Montfort, Francis of Assisi, the Good Thief, and
> St. Benedict Labré—all these names have been
> singing in my heart for almost twenty years.

How can any of us explain our attraction to one saint or
another? Could it possibly be that they that they are attracting us
and that it is not just we who find them attractive? I remember that,
when I was in my early twenties, I was fascinated by the Good
Thief, and in my book *Au coeur de la misère: la miséricorde* (In the
Midst of Wretchedness: Mercy) I devoted a chapter to him.
For a long time, I have wanted to write a book about the Good

Thief. I collected ideas, made notes, and then by mysterious circumstances Providence put Mr. Yves Carrer on my path; a layman from France who, for more than thirty years, has been working to make the Good Thief known and loved. He came to Quebec (Canada), we shared at length and I spoke to him about my project. He strongly encouraged me. He assured me that the time had come to write this book and that he would help me to do it with his documentation and ideas. This providential encounter brought France and New France together so that the holy Good Thief might be better known and reflected on in the Church! But why do I believe that the Good Thief should be a point of spiritual reflection?

Where sin abounds, grace will be even more abundant!

Our world is experiencing a crisis of hope. In its pastoral concern for the salvation of the world, the Second Vatican Council responded to this human distress by shedding light on *divine mercy*. St. Paul had already had a glimpse of the mystery that even when "sin has increased—grace has increased all the more" (Rom 5:20)[1]. Jesus in His mercy has always identified Himself as seeking for the wayward and lost: the straying sheep, the prostitutes and the prodigal sons. This was evidenced most dramatically on Calvary, in Jesus dying moments as he suffered between two criminals. This was then, and still is a scandalous reality for many "righteous people."

One of the greatest misfortunes of our day is not sin as such, but the loss of the very notion of sin. We tend to seek the emptiness of artificial paradises to find a soothing sense of freedom from feelings of guilt, feelings we consider to be harmful in themselves. But by avoiding guilt we turn away from the Divine Mercy that is waiting to manifest itself.

As it has often been in the history of the Church, "the signs of the times" confirm the vision and wisdom of Vatican II, and the witness of the saints—men and women who have become witnesses of the Divine Mercy.

In late 1997, Thérèse of Lisieux was proclaimed "doctor of the Church". She was a woman who had offered her life on behalf of great sinners, non-believers and atheists, and desired nothing more than to be seated at the table of sinners and share their fate so as to obtain mercy for them. Thérèse stands at the door of our atheism eroded world as an example. In our day Pope John Paul II beatified Sister Faustina Kowalska, who was also a great apostle of merciful love. Sister Faustina heard this message from the Lord ...

> *I want priests to proclaim my great mercy. I want sinners to come close to me without fear of any kind. The soul, be it like a corpse in full decay, be there, humanly speaking, no longer any remedy, is not so before God! The flames of mercy are consuming me. I am eager to pour them over souls. I am all love and all mercy. No sin, be it an abyss of abjection, will exhaust my mercy, for the more it is drawn upon, the more it increases. My daughter, speak to the entire world about my mercy. Tell the priests that their words will crush the most hardened sinners if they preach about my inexhaustible mercy.*[2]

It is a message of this Divine Mercy that is conveyed to us by the example of the Good Thief—it is most obvious! In one instant, mercy lifts him from the deepest abyss of moral decay to the highest level of holiness. He is a unique example in the history of salvation, becoming the first "canonized" saint, the first sinner to whom the gates of paradise were opened.

The experience of the Good Thief completely upsets our scale of values. For we see that God has no need of our natural virtues. All he needs is our emptiness and poverty so that we can receive and be filled with his mercy. He abhors self-complacency, but desires a childlike trust from us. He wants to pour his mercy, like an overflowing torrent, into our poverty. God takes pleasure in displaying his power in the weakness of little ones.

At the beginning of the twentieth century, God was pleased to give "little Thérèse" to the world as a model of such mercy. Alas! Sometimes we have tarnished her witness by presenting her teachings as something childish and insipid. That is why we must associate her spirituality with the spirituality of the Good Thief, for they are similar.

My only wish in writing these pages is to present the Good Thief, the only saint canonized by Jesus himself, as someone to be contemplated, known, and loved in our time. It is possible for the recognition of Thérèse of Lisieux as doctor of the Church to become an occasion to help us discover "the little way" of the holy Good Thief, whose life speaks to the thieves that we all are? This way of absolute trust in God's mercy restores the Good Thief to the place he deserves in Christian devotion.

With all the progress that has been made in scriptural studies, light will be shed on his place and his time will come. At a time when violence is rampant in the world, it is good to reflect on the Good Thief in relation to all of us who are spiritually blind and all the sinners who are sincerely repentant. This wounded world must learn all over again to say in all truthfulness: *"Kyrie eleison!"*

Chapter 1

The Good Thief in the Gospel

There is a wonderful message in the story of the Good Thief for any of us who may be wondering: "Why live? What is the good of living? Is there any hope?" The Good Thief plunges us into the heart of the gospel message.

He brings us back to the mystery of the crucified Jesus and reminds us that, in order to rise with him and be reborn with him in glory, we must, in some way, be crucified with him.

He takes us into a spirituality that, by contemplating Christ in his Passion and Death and Resurrection, restores the centrality and essential basis of the Christian faith which is the mystery of Redemption, of Good Friday and Easter. Such is the "mission" of the Good Thief.

Such a Great Adventure

Writing in 1937 Father Albert Bessières had this to say:

> *A great adventure! So great that the world knows no similar one! A brigand dying beside Christ, "canonized" by him – the first canonized saint of the New Testament—venerated by the Christian world in all rites: Latin, Greek, Armenian, in thousands of*

shrines, glorified by the Fathers of the Church, the ascetics and the mystics, on the same level as the greatest apostles.[3]

At the time not everyone would have shared such an admiration for a man who had been a brigand or criminal before meeting Christ. Evidently, this character of the gospel was not completely unknown to Christians. Depictions of Calvary in artistic master-pieces, in icons, in the stained-glass windows of churches, and paintings in museums served to remind people of this episode in the Passion of Christ.

But who really paid attention to the Good Thief? Yet in the late thirties someone was meditating on this event, no doubt one of the most beautiful and most instructive of the gospel, which is relevant to all of us? Through his meditation Cardinal Jules-Gérard Saliège, arch-bishop of Toulouse, attempted to break through the wall of silence that surrounded the "holy" criminal. Straightaway, he declared:

> *The Good Thief has been the great forgotten one. On Good Friday, we remembered him in the Savior's Passion. [...] But who celebrates this Mass and who recites this office? We are very far from giving him the place that the Fathers of the Church reserved for him. When we read them, we are somewhat dumfounded. So much eloquence! So much admiration!*

Among the Good Thief's "heroic" virtues, the cardinal noted his "humility"—

> *The Good Thief had the courage to be humble, to admit his wrongs sincerely, a courage so rare and in this case so superbly rewarded. When God finds humility in a soul, he can no longer hold back, he rushes there with the torrent of his grace.*

And he noted the Good Thief's significance for the Church:

Canonized by Jesus! "Truly I tell you; today you will be with me in Paradise." The Good Thief is a witness of God's merciful love. He speaks of repentance and trust in [our] century that is dying of injustice and which, in spite of everything, is stirred by a magnificent hope. To sinful souls, he shows something of the unfathomable depths of the Heart of Jesus.

Who are the "thieves"?

Who were the two thieves crucified with Jesus? St. Luke, the evangelist of "Christ's goodness of heart" (as Dante wrote) provides some information about them.

Two others also, who were criminals, were led away to be put to death with him. When they came to the place that is called The Skull, they crucified Jesus there with the criminals, one on his right and one on his left (Luke 23:32-33).

There was also an inscription over him, "This is the King of the Jews." One of the criminals who were hanged there kept deriding him and saying, "Are you not the Messiah? Save yourself and us!" But the other rebuked him, saying, "Do you not fear God, since you are under the same sentence of condemnation? And we indeed have been condemned justly, for we are getting what we deserve for our deeds, but this man has done nothing wrong." Then he said, "Jesus, remember me when you come into your Kingdom." He replied, "Truly I tell you, today you will be with me in Paradise" (Luke 23:38-43).

Matthew and Mark offer some supplementary information, but without differentiating between the two thieves:

Then two bandits were crucified with him, one on his

right and one on his left. Those who passed by derided him shaking their heads and saying, "You, who could destroy the temple and build it in three days, save yourself!" If you are the Son of God, come down from the cross." In the same way, the chief priests also, along with the scribes and elders, were mocking him, saying, "He saved others, he cannot save himself. He is the King of Israel; let him come down from the cross now, and we will believe in him. He trusts in God; let God deliver him now, if he wants to; for he said 'I am God's Son'." The bandits who were crucified with him also taunted him in the same way (Mt 27:38-44).

And with him they crucified two bandits, one on his right and one on his left (Mk 15:27).

Those who were crucified with him also taunted him (Mk 15:32).

Usually what we hear about these thieves gives us the impression that their story begins only with the crucifixion and that before the crucifixion they had seen or heard nothing about Jesus. The simple reading of the *titulus* (the inscription affixed to the cross above Jesus' head) would have been enough to inform them, *in extremis,* about Jesus' identity.

We could be justified in asking a few questions:

- Did the two criminals know Jesus before they were crucified?

- Had they already met him at the Praetorium?

- Had they heard the accusations made against him by "the leaders of the Jews"?

- Had they heard of his declaration before the Sanhedrin?

- What might their personal attitude towards him have
been?

We might do well to "discover" who they were and what they
might have known.

Who were these men? Highway robbers? Or zealots—people
vehemently opposed to the Roman occupation of Israel? Or were
they bandits as well as zealots?

Some authors believe that the two thieves were only "common
law" criminals, that is, simple brigands: *latrones*, as we read in the
Vulgate.[4] Others like Joseph Blinzer, one of the foremost specialists
on the Passion of Jesus, hold an opinion that is rather widely shared
today. It gives to the Greek word *lestes* the meaning of "agitator," or
"resistance fighter."

The term "thieves", *lestai*, is used in the original Greek and
lestes is the term used by John in referring to Barabbas. The meaning is almost certainly the same here, referring not to a brigand or
an ordinary delinquent, but to a political agitator, a guerilla or a
zealot,—of a militant fighter in the cause of liberating Israel from
Roman occupation. The Romans did not recognize that the perpe-
trators of such revolt, rebels against their rule had any civil status.
They did not even consider them *hostes*—enemies—but simply
brigands, delinquents that had to be suppressed. Thus in the trio,
necessarily condemned to death, no other punishment was possible
against such accusations—their leader (Barabbas) had unexpect-
edly been replaced by Jesus.[5]

Several commentators attempt to reconcile the divergent inter-
pretations of the identity of these "thieves". Fr. Bessières writes:

> *The two criminals crucified with Jesus are brigands,*
> *both thieves, opponents to the Roman occupation*
> *and murderers. Their type infested Palestine at the*
> *time of Jesus. Their feats were generally covered by*
> *political motives. Hatred for the Roman invaders*
> *culminated in murders, uprisings for the sake of free-*
> *dom. Houses of Jews whose patriotism was judged to*
> *be too weak were sacked. Once their exploit was*

accomplished, they would go underground and keep on living from smuggling and robberies.6

Msgr. Guy Gaucher, in turn, wonders:

Who were they, "common law" criminals or political characters? Ordinary brigands operating on the road from Jericho to Jerusalem, or zealots, men who attacked the occupation soldiers...? Or both? Hardened individuals like Barabbas? Members of the resistance? It doesn't matter! In the insulting language of the rebel who addresses Jesus, we grasp the fact that they were not choir boys.7

The Good Thief himself answered the question by declaring publicly, "For us, we are getting what we deserve for our deeds..." (Luke 23:41).

By these simple words, he acknowledged the extreme gravity of their deeds. His attitude illustrates St. Paul's words perfectly: "For one believes with the heart and so is justified, and one confesses with the mouth and so is saved" (Rom 10:10).

Sedition in the City: Rioters Arrested and Imprisoned

Let us imagine the events preceding the crucifixion as follows: A few days before the Jewish Paschal Feast, a riot breaks out in the city. Barabbas is the instigator aided by his accomplices. A murder is committed. A detachment from the Roman garrison is dispatched to the area and some of the rioters are arrested and led to prison.

What do the gospels say about this?

At that time they had a notorious prisoner, called Jesus Barabbas (Mt 27:16).

Now a man called Barabbas was in prison with the rebels who had committed murder during the insurrection (Mk 15:7).

> *This was a man [Barabbas] who had been put in*
> *prison for an insurrection that had taken place in the*
> *city, and for murder (Luke 23:19).*

These texts, in spite of their brevity, allow us to reap a harvest of information:

- According to Matthew, Barabbas is "a notorious prisoner." By using this term, the evangelist clearly indicates that Barabbas had certain notoriety in the eyes of his compatriots; they even considered him a popular hero, a celebrity.

- When Luke speaks of rebellion, and Mark, of insurrection, they clearly show that they were attempting to incite a popular uprising, a revolt against the established authority, against the Roman occupation.

- Mark tells us that Barabbas was not directly responsible for the murder committed during the insurrection. He attributes it to the "rebels," his partisans, his accomplices.

The synoptics tell us that following their arrest, Barabbas and his accomplices were taken to a prison, perhaps an obscure dungeon under the Antonia fortress—where the Roman garrison was stationed—to await their appearance before the imperial procurator to face charges of rebellion and murder.

In the Praetorium

The Praetorium, contrary to what some might think was not a judicial tribunal, but the palace where the governor resided when he came to Jerusalem for special events and festivities, especially the Passover. As a rule he lived at Caesarea, a city on the Mediterranean coast of northern Palestine that served as the capital of the province

During the time of Jesus, trials were carried out as follows:

The Roman custom was to speed up the trials one

after the other, beginning at dawn by gathering the people to be judged and putting them all together in the same room, where contradictors moved about. Thus it is certain that the two thieves were present at Jesus' trial, since they were judged and sentenced after he was. The Romans carried out death sentences without delay, on the very day of the trial.[8]

Pilate, surrounded by his assistants and with the help of an interpreter, would proceed with the interrogation of the accused in the auditorium, where the prosecutors as well as the praetorian cohort or personal guard of the governor also met. As for the tribunal itself, it was set up on a stage outside the Praetorium. It was there, at the place called *Lithostrôt*, *Gabbatha* (in Hebrew) that the procurator, from his curule chair facing the public, pronounced the death sentence.[9]

What the Criminals Heard at the Praetorium

On the day of the trial, the chief priests, the scribes and the elders, remained outside (so as to avoid ritual defilement in order to be able to eat the Passover) laid the charges against Jesus (John 18:28). The following charges, no doubt, seemed strange to our two accused men—"We found the man perverting our nation, forbidding us to pay taxes to the emperor, and saying that he himself is the Messiah, a king", they shouted furiously to the procurator (Luke 23:2).

Perplexed, Pilate listened ... so did the criminals! How could the two accused men not have been totally attentive to the one being tried ahead of them, and whose sentence would reveal the fate awaiting them?

Pilate returned to the Praetorium. It was time for the interrogation.

Matthew (27:11), Mark (15:2) and Luke (23:3) each pointed out the central question asked by the procurator, "Are you the king of the Jews?" and Jesus' reply, "You say so." John brings to this dialogue developments that bear the mark of his theology.

- Are you the King of the Jews?

- Do you ask this on your own, or did others tell you about me?

- I am not a Jew, am I? Your own nation and the chief priests have handed you over to me. What have you done?

- My kingdom is not from this world. If my kingdom were from this world, my followers would be fighting to keep me from being handed over to the Jews. But, as it is, my kingdom is not from here.

- So you are a king?

- You say that I am a king. For this I was born, and for this I came into the world, to testify to the truth. Everyone who belongs to the truth listens to my voice.

- What is the truth? (John 18:33-38).

When they heard this, the criminals must have been astounded; learning that effectively Jesus was king, yet not of an earthly kingdom of which they had perhaps dreamt, but of a kingdom that was not of this world. Astonishing![10]

Pilate grasped the fact that he was being confronted by a problem of a religious nature, in which he should not intervene. Indeed, Rome advised the governors, even ordered them to respect the religious customs and practices of the peoples under their authority. Pilate had to conform to this.

So returning to the terrace, and convinced of Jesus' innocence, he challenged the religious leaders and the crowd by declaring that he found no case against this man, no reason to condemn him, nothing that warranted his death. But the religious leaders insisted loudly, "He stirs up the people by teaching throughout all Judea, from Galilee where he began, even to this place" (Luke 23:5).

When he heard Galilee being mentioned, Pilate ordered Jesus

sent back to Herod Antipas, tetrarch of Galilee, who also was in Jerusalem for the Passover.

After he had been reviled, humiliated, jeered, insulted, outraged, beaten, clothed with the cloak of derision by Herod Antipas and his guards, Jesus was again brought before Pilate.

Pilate could still use a last resort to free Jesus—the Passover privilege. He was undoubtedly reminded of this by some of the people in the crowd. In fact, it was customary, on the occasion of the Passover, to grant the liberation of one prisoner, one whom the crowd desired to be released. Pilate. A high official had the right to free any accused man not yet tried.[11]

Pilate: "But you have a custom that I release someone for you at the Passover. Do you want me to release for you the King of the Jews?"

The crowd: "Not this man, but Barabbas!" (John 18:39-40).

Under the Roman panoply of penalties, scourging was a common punishment. Pilate therefore ordered this preventive penalty, hoping that he might thus satisfy the crowd.

After the torturous scourging Jesus was brought back to Pilate bruised, exhausted, covered with spit, his face disfigured, crowned with thorns, wearing a purple robe, carrying a reed in his right hand as a scepter. But Jesus' aspect, as pitiful as it was, had no effect on the crowd that had been manipulated into frenzy by their religious leaders. They roared all the more, "We have a law, and according to that law he ought to die because he has claimed to be the Son of God" (John 19:7).

The Great Conversational Topic of That Day

> Information travels rapidly in the Eastern world ...
> On the day of the preparation for the Passover or
> 'Parasceve', a single topic fed all the conversations:
> the astounding declaration Jesus had made before
> the Sanhedrin, a declaration by which—freely and
> royally—he had signed his own death warrant.

What do the evangelists tell us?

> *The high priest said to him, "I put you under oath before the living God, tell us if you are the Messiah, the Son of God." Jesus said to him, "You have said so. But I tell you, from now on you will see the Son of Man seated at the right hand of Power and coming on the clouds of heaven" (Mt 26:63-64).*

> *Again the high priest asked him, "Are you the Messiah, the Son of the Blessed One?"—Jesus said, "I am; and you will see the Son of Man seated at the right hand of the Power, and coming with the clouds of heaven" (Mk 14:61-62).*

> *When day came, the assembly of the elders of the people, both chief priests and scribes, gathered together, and they brought him to their councils. They said, "If you are the Messiah, tell us." He replied, "If I tell you, you will not believe; and if I question you, you will not answer. But from now on the Son of Man will be seated at the right hand of the power of God." All of them asked, "Are you, then, the Son of God?" He said to them, "You say that I am!" (Luke 22:66-70).*

These statements made by Jesus before the Sanhedrin under the chairmanship of Caiaphas, high priest for that year, were not simply a confirmation of his Messianic character. He was the Christ, the Messiah foretold and awaited as a liberator and Saviour of Israel— what Jesus really confirmed was his Divine Sonship. He was, properly speaking, the Son of God, a declaration which the Jews found blasphemous and deserving of death.

The thieves had possibly heard tell of this in the recesses of their cell, which undoubtedly was in the neighborhood of the Praetorium, and surely on the way to Golgotha. They were certainly wondering about the personality of the one with whom they were to be crucified, and they had a glimpse into the true motives behind his condemnation.

The words that the criminals used drew their inspiration from Jesus' answers to Pilate's questions. Here the three expressions they used ought to be noted:

- – Are you not the Messiah..." from the first thief.

- – When you come ..." an expression presupposing the faith of the Good Thief in Christ's glorious return.

- – "With your Kingdom" or "to inaugurate your Kingdom." In the mind of the dying Good Thief, this could not be about some earthly kingdom, but truly of this Kingdom of which Jesus had spoken and "which was not of this world."

Sentenced to Death according to the Roman law

Jesus' trial had just come to an end with a death sentence pronounced at the request of the Sanhedrin. While Barabbas was set free, Pilate had the reason for Jesus' condemnation drawn up: "Jesus of Nazareth, king of the Jews." Fr. Pierre Benoît, Director of the Biblical School of Jerusalem, notes that:

> *The basic agreement of the four evangelists about the inscription on the cross is most striking. All of them report the same expression: "King of the Jews." We truly felt this during the trial: this was the reason—Jesus' supposed claim to royalty, the accusation that the Jews presented to the Romans, although this was not their motive. It was not the title of king, but that of Christ, of Messiah, of Son of God, that was intolerable to them. Pilate understood very well that this political accusation was only a pretext, that this was certainly not about a revolutionary in the political sense, but he gave in. He*

accepted this "motive" of condemnation because it was the only one he could transfer to the archives and communicate to the emperor. "The accused claimed to be himself as king of the Jews." This detail of the ritual being fulfilled, there remained the judgment of the two thieves, who were undoubtedly accomplices of Barabbas.

It would have been surprising if Pilate had brought out only Barabbas to appear before the tribunal and had spared his accomplices – authors of the murder committed in the city during the uprising—who were in prison with him (according to Mark).

If the two thieves had been ordinary criminals of the "common law," they would have been brought before a local court to be judged. And in the event of a death sentence, the *exequatur* procedure, required to make the sentence enforceable, would have been followed. The death sentence would have had to be confirmed by the Roman governor who alone had the right to execute any of the provincial subjects under his authority. In the case of common criminality, the two thieves would have been put to death by stoning.

The sentence of crucifixion, according to Roman law, implies that they had appeared before a Roman court of law, the only authorized court to judge crimes of high treason, crimes against Romans and their sovereignty including troublemakers, rebels, dangerous criminals—in a word, all those who were a threat to the imperial order and whom the Romans considered as brigands (*latrones*).

The charges laid against them were, on the one hand, that they had participated in an uprising against Roman occupation and, on the other hand, that they had committed a murder in the process. These acts left them little likelihood of avoiding the ultimate sentence—crucifixion, and they were undoubtedly fully aware of this.

Pilate, who had full power as a governor of the order of the Roman Knights, was the supreme legal authority. One of the major responsibilities during his ten years as governor had been to pursue criminals. Therefore it was also his responsibility to either pronounce the death sentence against them after a rapidly executed trial in the wake of Jesus' trial, or again, after the declaration of their crimes by one of his assistants, who may have ordered the sentence without even an interrogation.

Pilate would certainly have hoped to get rid of Barabbas, who represented a real threat against himself and the occupation troops under his command. Moreover, the capture and execution of this notorious bandit would have gained him the esteem and gratitude of the emperor, thus fostering his political climb to power. Hence his great disappointment and keen annoyance, which can be detected in the sharp reply to the leaders of the Jews when they objected to the inscription signifying the condemnation of Jesus as the "King of the Jews"—"What I have written, I have written."

He found, in their objection, the ideal opportunity to ridicule the people by having their king, "King of the Jews", proclaimed on the *titulus* and accompanied by two criminals. "You will be crucified," he said curtly to each of the two brigands.

From then on, the two sentenced criminals each endured, in their own turn, the legal ritual torture: scourging, carrying of the *patibulum* (transversal beam of the cross), *and titulus* (inscription) tied to their neck, crucifixion and exposure in a busy location outside the walls of the city. And to finish them off—the breaking of their legs or *crurifragium*.

Dreadfully Scourged

Just as he had done with Jesus, Pilate handed the two criminals over to the military executioners who were in charge of seeing the death sentence carried out.

Under Roman law, anyone who was handed over to the soldiers to be scourged lost his status as a human being. He thus became merely an empty shell for whom the law no longer cared, a body that could be tortured without regard.

In certain cases scourging was the principal sentence, but for the two criminals as for Jesus it was just preliminary punishment preceding their crucifixion. The purpose of scourging was first to intensify their suffering and then to concentrate their agony toward death because of the ensuing exhaustion.

Like Jesus the two criminals undoubtedly suffered the kind of scourging in the Praetorium that was normally reserved for slaves. It was carried out with the use of *flagra*, lashes made up of strips of leather studded with metallic balls, or with scorpions or sharp metal points.[12]

How many blows were they given? While Jewish law prescribed that the number could not exceed thirty-nine, there was no restriction under Roman law: it completely ignored limitation or leniency. Once this torturous ritual was completed, the blood covered criminals joined Jesus in waiting for the appalling procession towards Golgotha to begin.

Quadroons of Roman soldiers, under the command of a centurion—known as the *exactor mortis*, waited for the procurator's orders: *I, lictor, expedi crucem*—"Go, lictor, prepare the cross!"

The Final Preparations

There was one last formality to fulfill before the order for the procession to begin could be given. Under Roman custom those condemned to crucifixion were required to carry on their back or chest, the *titulus,* a placard inscribed with the charge for which they were being condemned, and which was to be carried all the way from the tribunal to the place of execution.[13]

The placard was normally painted white and its inscription was red or black so as to be perfectly legible. The charges were written in three languages: in the local language (Hebrew or Aramaic); in the language of administration (Latin); and in the commercial language (Greek).[14]

The horizontal crossbeam or *patibulum* was also to be carried to the place of execution by the accused. Jesus and the two criminals with him were ordered to stretch out their arms. The soldiers then placed the heavy burden horizontally on their swollen shoulders, behind their necks, stretched their hands over the wood and bound them firmly to it with ropes.

The Pitiful Procession

The procession comprised of Jesus, the two criminals and the detail of soldiers ordered for this function by the *exactor mortis* was now ready. Through streets and alleys teeming with the townspeople of Jerusalem the procession wound its way slowly and painfully towards a new rampart built under Herod's rule. The rocky hillock that the gospels refer to as Golgotha was about a hundred meters away. Posts were already in place.

There were "a great number of people" (Luke 23:27) all along the way. If the crowd appears to have shown some compassion for Jesus, the same was not the case for the two criminals: a profusion of boos and jeers were probably directed at them. Indeed, according to Titus-Livius and Cicero, common custom allowed the crowd to accompany the sentenced offenders with whiplashes during the procession towards the place of execution.

In this crowd, there "were women who were beating their breasts and wailing for him" (Luke 23:27). Who were these women? A string of names comes to our mind: Mary Magdalene, Joanna, Suzanna, Martha and Mary of Bethany and the *thygateres Jerusalem*, ladies from wealthy families who fulfilled the role of "institutional hired mourners." They formed an association to help the unfortunate victims condemned to be crucified (*cruciarii*). They provided moral support by showing grief as described by the evangelist, as well as material aid by preparing a mixture of "myrrh and wine: (Mt 15:23). The latter had a narcotizing effect on the suffering condemned who drank of it.

At Golgotha

Crucifixion was of Persian origin and was inherited by the Romans from the Carthagians. Historians of the time considered it to be "the most atrocious death,"[15] "the ultimate of tortures," "the most cruel and terrible way of putting to death,"[16] "the torture reserved for slaves," according to Maximus, Tacitus, Valerius, Titus-Livius; finally, the most shameful death since the victim on the cross lost even his Roman status.

Golgotha,[17] that sinister place, was located outside the city near the gate of Ephraim. In fact, it was proper to give the event as much publicity as possible; so it had to be visible while it exercised a dissuasive effect. Also, the execution had to take place facing the people so they could attend this gruesome spectacle.

We can deduce from Mark's statement: "The centurion who stood facing him" (15:39) that the cross was probably not much higher than the stature of a man. The feet of the victims were usually about one meter above the ground.

Sometimes crosses were built with a seat to support the bodies of victims, but these also served to prolong their agony. This was probably not the case on that day on the Golgotha, as breaking the legs of the thieves would not necessarily have had an immediate mortal effect. The victims were held up by their arms on which there would have been a traction force of some 80kg; and by their feet which were pinned into place by means of a nail driven through them.[18]

As a final formality of crucifixion the soldiers had to fasten the placards (*titulus*) with the inscribed charges onto the vertical beam, just above the head of each victim.

The Problem of the Synoptics

The synoptics and John the evangelist point out that Jesus was crucified between two criminals, one on his right and the other on his left. They all referenced a historical event they knew. According to Matthew and Mark, the thieves added their voices to the insults and mockeries of the passers-by, of the chief priests, the scribes, the elders and the soldiers: "The bandits who were crucified with him also taunted him in the same way" (Mt 27:44) "Those who were crucified with him also taunted him" (Mk 15:32).

Luke states that "one of the criminals who were hung with Jesus kept deriding him." The evangelist even reports his words "Are you not the Messiah? Save yourself and save us!"

When we hear these words from one of the criminals, we ask ourselves: is this really an insult? It is possible that this could have been either a request or an insult, but the most obvious and natural meaning is the latter. Luke immediately relates the sharp rebuke that the Good Thief addresses to his companion in misery, "Do you not fear God, since you are under the same sentence of condemnation? And we indeed have been condemned justly, for we are getting what we deserve for our deeds, but this man has done nothing wrong."

But where, precisely, does the insult lie? Would it not be in the very form of the request, relating it to an insolent formal summons, rather than in its content?—or else in the fact that, through his insistence in joining in with the perfidious accusers of Jesus, the criminal ended up compromising himself along with them?

Father Lagrange considers the words of the "evil thief" to Jesus not as a confession of faith, but essentially a "brutal irony." In other words: "When someone claims to be the Messiah, he should solve his problems and those of his comrades as well!"

Commentators like Sohans, starting from *neque tu* in the Vulgate, have translated the thief's remark as:

> *"You have no fear of God, yet condemned as we are, you will appear before him." The Good Thief's rebuke seems to bear on this aggression against Jesus, rather than on the other thief's general disposition. The meaning would thus be: "You have no fear of God (and you allow yourself to attack him), because you are under the effect of the same condemnation, a ploy you are using to authorize yourself to bring him down to the same level as you are."*[19]

We may agree that the Good Thief might have also asked Jesus, in a fraternal way, to get himself as well as them out of their predicament; but that he would have insulted him appears unthinkable. Why? If that had been the case, the rather sharp rebuke he addresses to his companion would have been totally incongruous. This sudden turn around in this "tough" criminal, a man who was not devoid of personal pride – his declaration, which was likely made a short time after being nailed to the cross, when he still had enough strength to speak[20]—would have been absolutely incoherent and even humiliating.

Furthermore, supposing he had compromised himself just moments earlier when members of the Sanhedrin were still present, isn't it unimaginable that he would immediately turn around and show so much assurance in rejecting Jesus' death sentence and publicly proclaim his innocence?

"This man has done nothing wrong," he said. Should we be at all surprised by this thief's sudden concern for justice—a man who surely possessed a basic sense of honesty?

He must have discerned in Jesus some human and supernatural qualities that would have been unusual among his compatriots. He had also realized the degree to which the trial of Jesus had been a vulgar masquerade, a harrowing parody of justice. Had he not seen Pilate hesitating in how to proceed, how to come out of the dilemma in an honorable way? Had he not heard him declare that he could find nothing deserving of death in this man?

How unfortunate it would have been to know nothing about the words and attitudes of the two criminals, companions in Jesus' misery! Could we imagine it possible for them to have nothing to say during the long hours that they hung on their posts, without even expressing their feelings?—Without any reaction, in one way or another?

Some commentators state that the Good Thief, who did not know Jesus personally and who was certainly not a "theologian," could not make such a profession of faith. How could anyone who had heard the accusations of the chief priests, the governor's questions, and the replies of Jesus put forth such a hypothesis?

What great subject of conversation could possibly have captivated their attention all along the way to Golgotha, if not Jesus' astounding revelation before the Sanhedrin?[21]

"He was not a theologian!" Must one be a theologian to make a profession of faith in Christ? The Good Thief's faith was born out of his attraction to the person and words of Christ. It was for him a gift from God, a seed in his Spirit.

When God inspired the Lucan account of the Good Thief's conversion, was it not precisely for the purpose of manifesting the almighty power of his grace, his infinite patience and his unfathomable mercy for the greatest of sinners? If St. Paul gave such an interpretation to his own conversion (cf. 1 Tim 1:12-14), is not the Good Thief's witness all the more extraordinary?

Crurifragium: Agony, Death and Burial

Jesus died at the ninth hour (15:00). A delegation from the Sanhedrin rushed to Pilate to request that he apply the crurifragium (breaking of the legs) to the three crucified men. There were two reasons for this move:

- First, Deuteronomy (21:22-23) ordered that the remains of the dead be removed before sundown;

- Secondly, this was the day of Preparation. The bodies were not to remain on the cross during the Sabbath which began that evening and which was a day of great solemnity (John 19:32). But did they have to break their legs?

Origen, who was born in 185 was very knowledgeable concerning the customs of the Eastern World, and pointed out that Jewish tradition required a spear be driven under the arm pit, in the region of the heart, to hasten the death of the victim. This is precisely what the soldiers did to Jesus' corpse (*Tract. 35 en Mat.*). This means that the Sanhedrin's initiative asking Pilate to apply the *crurifragium* to the three crucified men ran counter to their own tradition.

"When evening had come" (Mk 15:42), that is shortly before 18:00, Roman soldiers arrived with iron clubs. They began by breaking the legs of the criminals, "of the first and of the other who had been crucified with him" (John 19:32). These criminals were thus deprived of the support offered by the nail, eighteen centimeters in length, driven through their feet. This hastened their death by asphyxiation. Then coming to Jesus and seeing that he was already dead, "they did not break his legs, instead one of the soldiers pierced his side with a spear and at once blood and water came out" (John 19:33-34). This would have been a pericardial fluid similar to water. John, who attended this whole scene, testifies to this: "He who saw this has testified so that you also may believe. His testimony is true, and he knows that he tells the truth" (John 19:35).

So before sundown and in order to respect the Sabbath, the bodies of the two thieves were removed from Golgotha along with the instruments of their torture. They were cast into the bottom of a cistern that served as a common grave near the place of their crucifixion, that is, outside the city, towards the valley of refuse, the gruesome Gehenna at the foot of Haceldama, nearby those who had preceded them "in shame."

For the Jews, the absence of a proper burial would have contaminated all Jerusalem and thus have made their fulfillment of the rites prescribed for the Temple, the home, the camps and the caravanserais impossible.

Moreover, if the corpse of one sentenced to death remained hanging on the cross after sundown, it would desecrate not only the living, but also the deceased buried nearby, including those crucified by a legal sentence (Deut 21:22 ...).

Finally, burial fulfilled a humanitarian feeling amongst the Jews, its absence being the equivalent of a cruelty that they judged to be excessive.

After the Jewish revolt led by Bar Kokheba, the emperor Hadrian (+ 134), who was determined to permanently obliterate all vestiges of Christianity, which was then expanding rapidly throughout the Roman empire, ordered that Calvary be covered with an enormous mass of earth and stones. The rocky hill where the executions had taken place was thus transformed into an immense platform on which the emperor subsequently had a temple built to the glory of Venus and Adonis. He even erected the statue of Jupiter on the very site of the Holy Sepulchre.

The result of all these activities was just the opposite of what the emperor wanted, since it made possible the location of Calvary and the identification of the site. Years later, St. Helena (255-328), mother of the emperor Constantine, had the site cleared. The sepulcher and the crosses of Jesus and the Good Thief were discovered and recognized by certain evidence. The empress ordered that Jesus' cross be brought to Constantinople. Later, she offered parts of the cross to the Christian community at Cyprus.

According to tradition, fragments of the Good Thief's cross were sent to Jerusalem, to Rome (the horizontal beam of the Good Thief's cross is venerated in the splendid basilica of the Holy Cross of Jerusalem), also to Bologna, in the basilica of Santo Stefano and in the church Santi Vitale and Agricola, and to many other places as well.

The Names Attributed to the Two Thieves

Before discussing the names which have been historically attributed to the two thieves crucified with Jesus, we must consider the use of the *titulus* by the Romans, a use confirmed by the evangelists. Matthew and John tell us that the *titulus* carried by Jesus (and therefore by the other two condemned men as well) indicated not only the charges against him but also his name: Jesus of Nazareth. St. John offers most interesting complementary details.

> *Pilate also had an inscription written and put on the cross. It read, "Jesus of Nazareth, the King of the Jews." Many of the Jews read this inscription, because the place where Jesus was crucified was near the city; and it was written in Hebrew, in Latin and in Greek. Then the chief priests of the Jews said to Pilate, "Do not write, 'The King of the Jews,' but 'this man said I am King of the Jews'." Pilate answered, 'what I have written I have written'"* (John 19:19-22).

In order for the public to see it, the placard with the inscription was nailed to the vertical beam, above the head of the condemned man, as Luke points out. It is therefore possible that the crowd may have known the names of the two thieves—even though the evangelists do not mention their names.

The *Acts of Pilate*, an apocryphal text from the second century, assigns the names Dismas and Gestas to the two thieves. The *Petits Bollandistes* speaks of St. Dismas, the Good Thief, and evokes the famous legend passed down from St. Anselm, about Jesus meeting this brigand when Mary and Joseph were fleeing to Egypt.[22] A stanza from the Middle Ages written in Latin verse says:

> *For different reasons, three bodies are hanging on*

the gibbet: Dysmas on one side, Gestas on the other, in the middle Almighty God. Dysmas goes up to heaven; Gestas goes down into the abyss. May the Sovereign Power preserve us, us and our possessions! Recite these verses so as not to be robbed of what belongs to you.

This work cites still other names according to the times and places: Matha and Joca; Lustin and Vissimus ...

Dismas, Disme, Dysmas, Dumas (possibly from the Greek Dysmé which means "dying man") as well as Matha and Lustin are variations which have no importance.

Today the name Dismas is not recognized as accurate as it rests on no certain proofs. Even though the name was used in ancient martyrologies—including that of Baronius, among others—and even though many shrines were erected in his name, the name "Dismas" has been officially ruled out.

The new Roman martyrology does not use a name and is satisfied with designating Jesus' companion in torture by the traditional name of "Saint Thief."

We may reflect in passing on the action of the Holy Spirit, who inspired Scripture. He has disposed everything so that the Good Thief may not be confined to the narrow limits of a name, but be presented to us in his state of being a "thief," or sinner—as we all are in various ways.

So this name, "thief" that is common to him and to us—confers a truly universal dimension on this first "canonized" saint in history. Is this not a call to place ourselves firmly in the wake of the one who is a leader among thieves: the holy Good Thief!

The Good Thief Today

During this crucial time in human history, there seems to be *a return to the cross of Christ.*

Can we see a reflection of ourselves in the traits of the Good Thief on the cross? Are we not crucified like him in physical and moral suffering? Are we not condemned to death as he was? Like him, are we not sinners?

The Good Thief as a witness of the bloody sacrifice on Calvary also helps us grasp the unfathomable mystery of Christ's Passover and to live out more fully our participation in the Eucharist. Born in the pain of Golgotha, this "firstborn" of the Church helps us come to a better understanding of the mystery of the Church.

May the "holy good thief" whose example was so strongly emphasized by the Fathers and doctors of the Church, inspire in us the desire to follow his own way: the rapid and sure way that leads us to the Merciful Heart of the crucified Jesus Christ, the Redeemer of the world!

May our hearts be filled with hope, for:

> *... we proclaim Christ crucified, a stumbling block to Jews and foolishness to Gentiles, but to those who are called [...] the power of God and the wisdom of God. For God's foolishness is wiser than human wisdom, and God's weakness is stronger than human strength ... But God chose what is foolish in the world ... what is low and despised ... to reduce to nothing things that are" (1 Corinthians 1:23, 24, 25, 27-28).*

The Good Thief and the Possibility of Conversion in the Modern World

In our sated Western societies, we sense very well what separates us from God, it is our rejection of death and our determination not to suffer. We have become very strong in the exercise of this rejection and determination. Basically, the modern world does not reject paradise; it wants it immediately and without paying the price for it. It wants paradise but it rejects the way that Christ has traced to reach it, so it adopts another paradise so as not to follow this way. It does not accept that paradise is beyond this world; it wants it on this earth, within the immediate reach and especially without any suffering thrown in. So it blasphemes the true paradise, it tramples the key. It thus reduces humanity to what it was before Christ: without God in this world and without real hope. The earthly paradise of our modern world is only an ersatz of a paradise that is transformed into a hell.

The true forgiveness of our modern world, the one that holds before it the prophetic mirror of its possible conversion, is the Good Thief, so close to the traditional Russian devotion.

– Truly I tell you; today you will be with me in Paradise!

It seems to me that Jesus could not state more clearly that, from the moment we are on the cross, the key is already introduced into the lock of Paradise, provided of course that this cross is accepted.

Let us never forget that the only saint canonized by Jesus Christ was a highway robber, justly punished for his crimes. But he heartily accepts his punishment and his suffering and his death, because he has sensed that the cross on which he is nailed is the very key of the paradise of which his neighbor in torture is the Lord.

R. L. Bruckberger
La Révélation de Jésus Christ, Grasset

Chapter 2

The Early Church Fathers and the Good Thief

A review of the writings of the early Church Fathers and the doctors of the Church reveals many surprising references to the Good Thief. They are virtually unanimous in their admiration for the Good Thief to the point of making one wonder about the reason behind such effusiveness, such a keen interest?

Exhaustive research in patristic writings reveals the extent to which the example of the good thief has been the object of meditation and commentary. Among others is one Father of the Church who did not hesitate in making the following declaration during a Paschal homily:

> *What king would accept to have an outlawed criminal by his side to share his triumph? The king of Heaven, who has been victorious over death, enters his Kingdom in the company of a bandit! Mercy loves to play big game.*

Church Fathers of the Third Century

Origen

Originally from Alexandria, Origen died in about 240 AD and is still considered to be one of the greatest geniuses of the Church: a universal theologian, he was the author of many works. The goal of his allegorical exegesis was to help us make the transference between the literal meaning of Scripture and the spiritual meaning.

He describes the Good Thief as

> ... *the figure of those who, after many sins, believed in Christ and said: "We are bound with Christ on the cross and similar in death." They always say to the Son of God: "Remember me when you come into your Kingdom!" and are subsequently with him in paradise.*[23]

On the dogmatic level, this means

> ... *that it is sometimes possible to obtain justification already only for having believed and done absolutely nothing. We may, for example, cite the one who was justified by faith alone, without works, the brigand crucified with Jesus.*[24]

Origen applied the words of St. Paul in his letter to the Romans to the Good Thief: "Then what becomes of boasting? It is excluded. By what law? By that of works? No, but by the law of faith. For we hold that a person is justified by faith apart from works prescribed by the law" (Rom 3:27-28).

Less than anyone, the Good Thief could never have relied on his own merits. The only thing he had was his faith in Christ, who, operating out of love, enabled him to attain justice and holiness.

Cyprian of Carthage

Cyprian was originally a lawyer from Carthage and following his conversion he became first a priest and eventually the bishop of this city. His holiness, his knowledge and his firmness made him one of the greatest bishops during the first centuries of the church and he exercised great influence throughout the Church. Because of persecutions, he withdrew from Carthage for a period of time, but then he decided to return in order to bear witness to Christ. For this he was beheaded, dying in the presence of his faithful on 14 September 258.

For Cyprian there was no doubt that the Good Thief had been baptized in his own blood and that his blood was that of a martyr.

During the passion of the thief, we must distinguish between two phases—two men—two bloods. The blood that he shed before he had faith was the blood of a thief; upon coming to faith his blood was that of a Christian. And the blood he then poured out—was a testimony to the Christian faith, confirming the divinity of the Son of God – it was the blood of a martyr.[25]

Cyprian goes back to this statement on several occasions:

Having become familiar with Christ, his confession makes him Jesus' colleague in martyrdom. The Good Thief exchanges the cross for paradise and the punishment for homicide makes him a martyr.[26]

Cyprian proposes the example of the Good Thief as a priority to the world of those who suffer:

Those who are baptized in their own blood and sanctified in their passion obtain perfection and the grace of the divine promise. The Lord declares this himself when he speaks to the thief who believes in him and confesses him in his own passion: he promises him that he will be with him in Paradise.[27]

On the level of pastoral work for the sick, it is especially important to emphasize this passage from St. Cyprian's letter:

Those who are sanctified in their passion, that is, in
the suffering inherent in their illness, infirmities, old
age, certain situations, obtain perfection and accede
to holiness. They therefore obtain, as the Good Thief
did, the grace of the divine promise: "Today you will
be with me in Paradise."[28]

Church Fathers of the Fourth Century

Hilary of Poitiers

Hilary, Bishop of Poitiers, sustained a merciless struggle against
the Arians who denied the divinity of Christ. Emperor Constance,
who favored the Arians had Hilary exiled to Asia Minor. When he
eventually returned to Poitiers, he committed all his strength to the
defense of the true faith and prior to his death in 38 he had
succeeded in freeing Gaul from the Arian heresy. Pope Pius IX
proclaimed him doctor of the Church.

On the subject of the Good Thief, Hilary, like Origen, highlighted the theme of justification by faith:

*The one on the right is saved by justification of
faith.*[29]

And in the wake of Cyprian, he claims the glorious title of
martyr for the Good Thief.

Ambrose of Milan

After brilliant studies in law, Ambrose was named governor of
Northern Italy and prefect of Milan in 372. Two years later, at the
request of the people, he was chosen to become the Bishop of Milan
in spite of the fact that he was not yet baptized. Baptized on 30
November 374, he was consecrated Bishop on 7 December.

Sustained by the emperors, he was a fearless defender of the
Catholic faith against Arian heresy. He was an excellent orator and
his sermons were instrumental in Augustine's conversion. Ambrose

died on 4 April 397.

Commenting on Jesus' promise of Paradise to the Good Thief and on its geographical location, Ambrose used an expression that has continued to resound in the Church:

> *A magnificent testimony that we must work at our conversion, since forgiveness is so readily granted to the Good Thief and grace is bestowed more abundantly than prayer! The Lord always gives more than what we ask, for life consists in being with Christ. Wherever Christ is, there is the Kingdom.*[30]

Athanasius of Alexandria

Athanasius was chosen by the people as bishop of Alexandria. For almost fifty years, he fought to defend the faith against Arianism. He continued his work in spite of five periods of exile before his death in 373.

During a sermon for the Parasceve, he let his admiration and his affection for the Good Thief burst forth. He pointed out his faith and charity and conferred on him the title of evangelist:

> *O Good Thief, much shrewder than the first Adam! Poorly advised, he reached out for the fruit of the forbidden tree and infused in himself and in all of us the venom of death. Better advised, by reaching out to the sacred Tree of the cross you recovered Heaven and earned Life! O blessed thief, who found the means of carrying off the most wonderful treasure! O blessed thief who imitated Judas's betrayal, but the one betrayed was the devil! O blessed thief, who made the cross an eloquent pulpit from which, with superhuman energy, you undertook to defend your Redeemer! O blessed thief, who showed everyone the power of faith, the effectiveness of a well-made confession and sincere repentance.*[31]

Cyril of Jerusalem

Cyril became Bishop of Jerusalem around 350 AD and exercised his ministry for thirty-six years during a period troubled by consecutive schisms resulting from the heresies of Arius. He was exiled for sixteen years. In 381 he participated in the Council of Constantinople. He died in 386. Twenty-four of his catecheses have been preserved and they constitute a precise testimony of the doctrinal teaching of the Church during the middle of the fourth century. He was also named a doctor of the Church.

> *O Good Thief, what power has enlightened you? Who taught you to adore a man held in contempt, crucified with you? O eternal Light that gives light to the blind. It is right for you to hear these words: "Have faith!" Not that your works could inspire you to have trust, but the King is there, the one who gives grace.*[32]

Gregory of Nyssa

A spiritual theologian of the Church and Bishop of Nyssa in Cappadocia, he participated with Gregory of Nazianzus in the Council of Constantinople in 381. He died in 394.

> *This skillful and inspired thief notices a treasure and wisely takes advantage of the opportunity. He took possession of the treasure of eternal life. A praiseworthy and admirable use of the art of thieving.*[33]

Church Fathers of the Fifth Century

John Chrysostom of Constantinople

As Bishop of Constantinople, John distinguished himself by his kindness towards the unfortunate, by his courage before emperors, and through his eloquent preaching which earned him the name "Chrysostom" (golden mouth).

John was an ardent defender of the truth. His many writings earned him the title of "Doctor of the Church". He died in 407 as a result of the mistreatment he endured during two periods of exile.

John Chrysostom was one of the most zealous advocates of the Good Thief. His writings greatly influenced Byzantine liturgy and, ever since that time, the Good Thief has occupied an eminent place beside Christ, the Redeemer in the liturgy. *De Cruce et Latrone* is a brilliant treatise on the power of the cross of Christ, which offers back the lost paradise to everyone.

On Mercy

> *Christ chose the summits of iniquities for his ulti-mate pardons so that we would have no excuse for despairing.*[34]

> *No one, henceforth, will be able to despair about his salvation when he sees a man guilty of thousands of sins cross the gates of the Kingdom. With a simple word, a single act of faith, he bounds ahead of the apostles into paradise; to lead us to understand that good deeds are not what earned him this favor, but the philanthropy of the Lord, who did everything. Did he fast? Did he shed tears? Did he do a lengthy penance? Not at all! But by a simple word, he found salvation on the cross itself. See how rapidly he goes from the cross to heaven, from torture to salvation!*[35]

> *The Good Thief is the obvious proof that God's*

mercy opens access to salvation to everyone ... An incomparable wonder of divine mercy! Mercy is what accomplished everything. Note the speed! ...[36]

Because of the Cross

The Good Thief, who had neither heard prophecies nor seen miracles, and who now sees Christ bound to the cross, does not stop at the dishonor. He does not see the ignominy; he sees the divinity and cries out: "Remember me in your Kingdom."

This is because the cross itself is the symbol of the Kingdom. If I call Christ "King," it is because I see him crucified. This is the proper fate for a king: to die for his subjects.

It is when he is nailed to the cross, stricken with insults, covered with spit, outraged, ridiculed, when he has become the object of universal derision that he has the power to draw to himself the perverted soul of the thief. Admire this power that bursts forth on every side: he unsettles nature, shatters rocky boulders, and the soul of the thief, that is more hardened than rocks, is made softer than wax.

The Lord performs two miracles on the cross: he opens heaven to humanity and introduces a thief there: "Today you will be with me in Paradise." What are you saying? Crucified, you promise heaven! Yes, and so that the infinite power I enjoy in the cross may burst forth. I have wanted this miracle, an unparalleled monument to my power, not only while I raised the dead, but while I was being heaped with insults. It was then that I wanted to change the thief's soul, more hardened than rocks.[37]

On the Faith of the Good Thief

Heroism of faith: I claim that it was greater than that of the patriarchs, of the prophets, than that of Abraham and of Moses, than that of Isaiah and

Ezekiel ... I mean to show that the Good Thief's faith was superior.[38]

He saw God only in the ignominy of the cross.[39]

You ask me, what did he do that was so great to deserve paradise immediately after his death. You want me to sum up his titles? Whereas Peter denied his Master, the Good Thief professed his faith in him on the cross. The first could not bear the threats of a humble servant girl; and the thief on the gibbet, surrounded by blaspheming people, proclaimed what his righteous soul could see with the eyes of faith: the divinity of the King of Heaven!

Give me a thousand servants faithful to their master while he is enjoying his fortune, and a servant who, in the time of trial, does not leave his master while a thousand others abandon him. Will the first be considered as much as the second when prosperity returns? No, surely not! Patriarchs, prophets, apostles, martyrs, you have believed in the Lord, you bound yourselves to him because you saw him at the peak of his glory, as he performed his miracles; but the Good Thief saw him only in ignominy and he remained faithful to him.[40]

On His Conversion

He continues his trade as a thief. He saw a rich man, bearer of treasures of Divine Wisdom and, according to his habit; he robbed him to enrich himself with his plunder.[41]

Whom can you find more miserable than this thief? And all of a sudden, here he is the most fulfilled man! When he is led to the cross and death, everyone is condemning him, his life is coming to an end, this life that was but one crime. But, for having opened his soul for one moment to the fear of God, here he is in the rank of the blessed.[42]

On His Confession

He did not say "Remember me" before he had rejected the burden of his sins through his confession. The thief begins by confessing, by laying down the burden of his sins. See what a great thing confession is! He confessed, and Heaven was opened; he confessed, and received from that such a great trust that he, a thief, dared claim the Kingdom![43]

On His Apostolate

The thief struggles against the thief, his companion. He says: "Up to this moment when we have been nailed on the cross, we have been in agreement and have worked together. But since the cross, I have changed paths. If you wish, walk with me towards Life, come! If not, go your own way!"[44]

On His Titles

Did you admire his philosophy in the midst of his tortures, his philosophy full of wisdom and doctrine? The thief not only was not shocked, but drew from the cross the arguments of a sublime philosophy. Rising above human appearances, carried up to heaven on the wings of faith, he philosophizes on eternity, and he affirms this crucified man, God, he thinks of his Kingdom. His philosophy scans future realities.

Is there a king who, upon entering triumphantly in his capital, would make a public thief sit by his side? Well! Our Lord did this! When he returned to his divine Homeland, he brought a thief with him ... Let us not forget, I pray you, this Good Thief! Let us not be embarrassed for receiving as doctor the one Our Lord was not ashamed to introduce as the first one to be with him in Paradise.

> *Before asking anything for himself, the Good*
> *Thief attempted to convert his companion. This thief*
> *became a prophet.*[45]

On His Canonization

> *You will find no one earning the promise of paradise*
> *before the Good Thief, neither Abraham, nor Isaac,*
> *nor Jacob, nor Moses, nor the prophets, nor the*
> *apostles. You find the thief ahead of all of them.*[46]

Jerome

Jerome was born in Dalmatia around 340. After studies in Rome, he was baptized, traveled to Gaul and then to Syria where he studied Hebrew and was ordained to the priesthood. Back in Rome, at the request of Pope Damasus, he translated the Bible into Latin. In 385 he returned to Palestine where he settled in Bethlehem, and devoted the rest of his life to the translation of the Bible (Vulgate). His scriptural works earned him the title "Doctor of the Church". He died between 415 and 420.

On the Martyrdom of the Good Thief

> *The thief exchanged the cross for paradise and, out*
> *of the punishment for his murders, he makes himself*
> *a martyr.*[47]

Augustine of Hippo

Augustine was born in Tagaste (Northern Africa) in 354. From his mother, St. Monica, he received a Christian education, but Augustine abandoned Christ to lead a life that was anything but edifying.

His meeting with St. Ambrose, bishop of Milan, was instrumental in bringing him back to God. He was baptized in Milan on Easter Day 387AD. When he returned to Africa, he was ordained to the priesthood and, at 41 years of age, was selected as Bishop of Hippo. During his thirty-six years as bishop, he fought against heresies.

On the Good Thief's Conversion

Blessed, blessed thief who is not held back by his usual thefts along the road, but takes possession of the way that is Christ, and in the wink of an eye is enriched with the true life.[48]

On His Faith

What had the thief done that is so great? Would you like me to tell you? While Peter was denying down below, he was confessing up above. He was not moved by the vociferating multitude that surrounded him. Those who had seen the Lord raising the dead wavered. The thief believed in him. I do not know what could be added to such a faith. Truly, the Lord has never found such a faith in Israel, or in the entire world.[49]

He believed in his heart and confessed with his lips.[50]
The thief was not crucified for the sake of Christ, but for his crimes; he did not suffer for having believed, but he believes at the moment he is suffering.[51]

On His Baptism

It is through the ineffable power and justice of the sovereign God that baptism was imputed to the believing thief and that he was judged as if he had received in his free spirit what he could not receive in his tortured body.[52]

The thief received the baptism of substitution not through the passion for the sake of Christ, but through the faith and conversion of the heart, taking into account that circumstances made it impossible for him to celebrate the sacrament.[53]

On His Martyrdom

> *Cyprian places him, and rightly so, among the martyrs. He earned as much merit for having confessed the crucified Jesus, as if he had been crucified for Jesus. The greatness of his martyrdom is measured in this way: he believed in Christ while the future martyrs were betraying Jesus.*[54]

On His Canonization

> *The thief is the only man who was totally assured of his predestination, an assurance based on an oath pronounced by God: "Truly I tell you; today you will be with me in Paradise."*[55]

Maximus of Turin

A contemporary of Augustine, Maximus of Turin presents the Good Thief's faith and especially his love for Jesus on the cross:

> *He believed that the crucified Jesus was glorified rather than punished. In this consists the model for the whole salvation: acknowledging the Savior as Lord of majesty from the very moment when we see him subjected to the sufferings of humility?*[56]

Leo the Great

Born in Rome at the end of the fourth century, he became Pope in 440AD under the name of Leo I.

In 451, he convened the Council of Chalcedon, which established the Christian dogma of the unity of the person of Christ in the duality of his natures: Christ is both God and man at the same time.

We still have about a hundred of his sermons addressed to the people of Rome and close to two hundred doctrinal letters that earned him the title "Doctor of the Church". Leo died in 461 AD.

On the Faith of the Good Thief

> *Who has instructed you? What words have given you*

this faith? What preacher this charity?[57]

Since the resurrection of the dead, the healing of the sick, the recovery of sight by the blind had ceased, and he did not know of the miracles that were about to burst forth. Still he proclaims his companion in torture Lord and King.[58]

The Good Thief's Titles

As we study the writings of the Fathers and the doctors of the Church, we discover that many titles are given to the Good Thief. The titles express the Father's true predilection for him.

"Master in philosophy, doctor, advocate for Jesus, figure and precursor of all the elect, prince of God, prophet," tells us a great deal about what St. John Chrysostom thought of the Good Thief.

"Doctor of charity," St. Augustine goes on; "evangelist," St. Athanasius of Alexandria goes one better.

We could go on—these are a true litany!

And those conferred by saints: "First fruit of all the elect, their figure, he is prince of Heaven, comforter of Jesus and comforter of Mary" according to St. Bernardino of Siena. "Cedar of paradise, resplendent star of heaven," for St. Peter Damian.

Ecclesiastical writers do not lag far behind: "He is a heavenly angel with huge wings. His flight bears him up to paradise," according to Athanasius the Sinaite.[59] "He is the doorkeeper of paradise" for Proculus of Jerusalem. "Firstborn of the despairing" for Arnaud of Chartres.[60] "Firstborn son of the crucified Christ, martyr, apostle, preacher of the universe, for, from the pulpit of the cross, he preached Christ to the whole universe, archangel of paradise, seraphim" for Cornelius a Lapide.[61]

These titles—which may seem to us somewhat exaggerated—set forth in a wondrous way the important place, even a dominating one beside the crucified Jesus Christ in the minds of the early Church Fathers, the Saints, and many great spiritual writers.

Meditation on the Holy Good Thief: A Prayer

O holy Good Thief, you are the only one among all the repentant great saints to have been canonized by Christ himself. Because of the sincere confession you made to him on the tribunal of Calvary and of your true repentance while you were hanging on the cross beside him in this open confessional, you were assured a place in heaven with Jesus on the very day of your death. By your sudden repentance and love, you opened the Heart of Jesus to mercy and forgiveness, even before the centurion pierced him with his spear. Your head was closer to that of Jesus, in his final agony, even closer than that of his beloved mother, the Virgin Mary, to offer him a word of comfort. You who knew how to pray so well teach us the words we should tell him to obtain our forgiveness and the grace of perseverance. You who are now so close to him in heaven, as you were in his last moments on earth, pray to him for me so that I may never abandon him. Pray to him so that at the end of my life I may hear the words he addressed to you then: "Today you will be with me in Paradise."

Nihil obstat: Paul Lacouline
Official censor
Imprimatur: Geo. E. Grandbois, v.g.
Quebec, 20 November 1954.

Chapter 3

The Mystery of the Cross

"Who is God to love us so much? Who is God, so destitute, so great, so vulnerable?" says a hymn. How can we speak of the mystery of the cross without speaking of the poverty and the innocence of the crucified God?

Speaking of the crucified God, Maurice Zundel writes:

> *The true God is that God who prefers to die rather than impose anything. God preferred to be crucified rather than take away from us the glory of making choices. God can be overcome; he is so on the cross where he dies of love for those who refuse eternally to love him. Anyone can kill him, for he is defenseless, he is disarmed like the candor of the eternal childhood. There is a childhood in God, an infinite fragility. What he asks from us is to empty ourselves from self because he is eternally emptied of self.*[62]

Who, more than the Good Thief, is poor and emptied of self like a defenseless child? He offers himself in his poverty, crucified next to the innocent Love. Christ on the cross appears to us in the total weakness of Love, and the vulnerability of God, and what we could call his eternal "agony." It is not by chance that Jesus dies as a "criminal" and opens paradise to a thief.

In these lines by Bernanos, we think of the Good Thief, of his life and death:

> *We really want what He wants, we really want, without being aware of it, our woes, our suffering, our solitude, while we imagine we only want our pleasures. We imagine we fear our death and shy away from it, when we really want this death as He willed his own. In the same way that He sacrifices himself on every altar where Mass is being celebrated, He starts dying all over again in each agonizing man. We want all that He wants, but we are not aware that we want Him, we do not know what we are, sin makes us live on the surface of ourselves. We will reenter our self only to die, and that is where He is awaiting us.*[63]

God is waiting for us on the cross, with arms outstretched and an open heart. At the foot of the cross it is impossible for us to doubt the powerful tenderness of the Heart of God. His Life is truly committed to our lives even to the point of dying on the cross. When we grasp the mystery of the crucified Jesus, we understand that God is not the one who makes us die, but that He is the *One who dies* with us, the guilty ones so that the guilty ones may rise from the dead with Him.

This is what the Good Thief understood.

The Good Thief, a Remedy

The revival of a devotional focus on the Good Thief meets with a need that is particularly urgent for Christians today, and offers a remedy for certain errors and deviations of our time. What the contemporary mindset rejects above all and excludes absolutely is the mystery of Redemption by the cross.

Glorification by the Cross

When he speaks of Jesus' glorification, John the evangelist is not using the term, as we might believe, to designate the resurrection or the ascension of Jesus, but His very *crucifixion*. In other words, it is in the cross itself, and there first of all, that John's inspired gaze sees His glory.

And such is the answer that the Holy Spirit proposes to those who eagerly covet glory and who find the cross to be a stumbling block.

Saint Thérèse-Benedicte de la Croix (Edith Stein) wrote:

The cross is the means of salvation that the unfathomable wisdom of God invented. God opens the floodgate of fatherly mercy to all those who have the courage to embrace the cross and the One who is bound to it.

The Holy Spirit enables us to discover this manifestation of glory in the cross. Eternally, and for the glory of the Most High, the cross brings striking proof of *the greatest love*— the love of the Father "who so loved the world that he gave his only Son" (John 3:16)— the love of the Son "who sacrificed himself" for his brothers. It is first the cross, before he was seated on the throne of the Kingdom, that the Son of man was exalted: "When I am lifted up from the earth, I will draw all people to myself" (John 12:32).

The Cross: An Inexhaustible Source of Grace

The Good Thief gives us a lesson of primary importance so that we may see in the cross of Jesus Christ a source of grace and holiness. These compensate superabundantly for and submerge the malice of all vice and crime, and transform in an instant the greatest criminal into a great saint. Therein lies the very mystery of the Redemption, the basis for all our Christian faith.

Jean Daujat wondered:

Why was the Good Thief really transformed in an instant from a great criminal into a great saint, whereas for us, the same infinite source of grace and holiness takes so many years to transform us little by little and make us holy?

The Good Thief was totally rejected, abandoned, held in contempt by men. He was, in himself and in the minds of all creatures, absolute spiritual poverty. So he could truly say before Jesus' cross: "O Cross, my unique hope." Never did the word "unique" take on such an absolute, rigorous and exclusive meaning. He, who had nothing of any worth to present to Him, hoped only for a pure gift, for pure generosity on the part of the Savior, for he could receive everything only from Jesus' cross. This is why he would be glorified eternally everywhere Jesus' cross would be glorified. The Good Thief, who completely lost faith in everything that is human or earthly, placed his sole hope in Jesus' cross and excluded everything else.[64]

Our contemporary culture no longer wants the cross, no longer preaches the cross, and this is why we so greatly need the teaching of this "little way" of the absolute poverty of the Good Thief.

Mystery of Helplessness

The mystery of the cross is the destitute and vulnerable love and innocence in absolute humility and poverty. Is not the cross of Christ the scandal of Love? Are we not too familiar with this folly of love and weakness?

The cross is not an effort of the will or a kind of stoic morality; it is weakness and poverty, the transfigured weakness that is revealed to the Good Thief on Calvary. Bernard Bro said:

The cross is not a mystery of power, but a mystery of helplessness. The cross is not a mystery of heroism, but a mystery of love. It does not consist in suffering with courage, but in being afraid to suffer; it does not consist in overcoming an obstacle, but in being crushed by it. Neither does it consist in being great and generous, but lowly and ridiculous in one's own eyes; nor in displaying virtue, but in seeing all one's virtue being ruined and reduced to dust, and in accepting all that in love.

And power is useless in accepting helplessness out of love; there must be love. So it is not solely through our will or by tightening our jaws that we will manage this. For if we are able to tighten our jaws, this means we are strong, and as long as we are strong—of that kind of strength—we do not know yet what the cross is. It is not a matter of being strong in a trial, but of being humble and disarmed enough for love to triumph in our lives.[65]

He Draws Everyone to Himself

"No one," Jesus said, "can come to me unless drawn by the Father who sent me" (John 6:44). It is therefore on the cross, that "he draws all people to himself" (John 12:32), revealing to us the true face of the Father of mercies. It is when he is crucified, arms stretched out on the cross, that the words addressed to Philip, "Whoever has seen me has seen the Father" (John 14:9) acquire their most powerful meaning. When we see Jesus crucified, we "see" the Father. In the innocence of the Crucified the face of the Father, who draws us to himself, is revealed. As Pope John Paul II said:

It is in Jesus crucified that we must see, according to the expression of the letter to the Colossians (1:15), the living image of the Father, the perfect icon of the invisible God, the revelation of mercy. In the Paschal mystery, Christ reveals the face of the Father to man and reveals man fully to himself.[66]

The Father, through the crucified Jesus, wishes to reveal his face to all the thieves of the world, in order to offer them his mercy and his forgiveness.

Offering One's Sufferings and Wounds

To partake in the cross of Jesus Christ we must, like the Good Thief, accept and offer up, out of love, everything that circumstances have allowed in life—everything that Providence, who wants only our sanctification and our greatest good, has permitted us by way of suffering, pain, rejection, sacrifice, humiliation and failure in life, including our more or less wounded childhood. Everything can be of use in our sanctification.

And because there is no other source of sanctity except the crucified Jesus Christ, there is no other way to holiness except the way of the cross, this *little way* of the Good Thief who was hung on the cross as was Jesus. Those who turn away from the way of the cross, turn away from holiness by shutting themselves out from the only source that is the crucified Jesus.

The Church needs to rediscover the efficacy of the cross, otherwise all our pastoral work will merely be a worldly humanism and our works nothing more than "resounding cymbals." And in spite of all our activities we will do no good and, at times, even do more harm than good.

At a time when the world wants a new kind of spirituality, a new Christianity without the cross, God continues to seek out *thieves* and transform them. In his book, *The Peasant of the Garonne*, the great Christian philosopher Jacques Maritain speaks about the death of an assassin:

> *When we meet a sinner we should be seized with great respect, as in the presence of one condemned to death—who can live again, and have in paradise, close to Jesus, a higher place than we. As I write these lines I have before me the memento of Jacques Fesch, "born on Passion Sunday, April 6, 1930, condemned to death on April 6, 1957, on the eve of Passion Sunday, executed at dawn, October 1,*

1957." He had come back to God in prison. In his last letters we find the following: "The nails in my hands are real, and the nails accepted. I understand better all the purity of Christ contrasted with my abjection. Since I accept wholeheartedly the will of the Father, I am receiving joy after joy" (August 16). "The execution will take place tomorrow morning, about four o'clock in the morning; may the will of God be done in all things ... Jesus is very near to me. He draws me closer and closer to him, and I can only adore him in silence, wishing to die of love ... I await love! In five hours I will see Jesus! He draws me gently to him, giving me that peace which is not of this world ..." A little later he observes: "Peace has left me and given place to anguish; my heart is bursting in my breast. And then: "I am calmer now than a moment ago, because Jesus promised me he will take me straight to Paradise, and that I will die as a Christian ... I am happy, farewell." (Night of September 30 to October I, the sixtieth anniversary of the death of St. Thérèse of Lisieux.)[67]

The Second Vatican Council speaks of the cross and of its mystery:

As Christ carried out the work of redemption in poverty and oppression, so the Church is called to follow the same path to communicate the fruits of salvation to men ... The Church ... is not set up to seek earthly glory, but to proclaim, by her own example, humility and self-denial ... The Church, however, clasping sinners to her bosom, at once holy and always in need of purification, follows constantly the path of penance and renewal. The Church ... "presses forward amid the persecutions of the world and the consolations of God, announcing the cross and death of the Lord until he comes" (Lumen Gentium, n° 8).

What pastoral message today still speaks of the cross of Christ? We must explain to Christians the meaning of their Christian life in the light of the cross. Followers of Christ are constantly confronted and seduced by the pleasures of the world, the thirst for power and wealth, and the resistance of their own flesh. The latter condemns them to a relentless struggle to safeguard the life of Christ; their earthly itinerary will never be a place of total rest.

In the disarray of our time, characterized by the unilateral exaltation of a naturalistic humanism, we are often afraid to speak of the "world" as St. John spoke of it. St. John spoke of a world dominated by the "prince of darkness", the out-and-out enemy of Christ, opposed to everything God-related. This world, for which the preaching of the cross is an absurdity and a stumbling block, is the world that is overcome by Christ.

Choosing the Way of the Cross

Nothing is more destructive to the very essence of Christianity than to imagine Christian life without the cross where, instead of relying on it alone, we would rely on our personal achievement. We would then be among those of whom St. Paul said, "For many live as enemies of the cross of Christ; I have often told you of them, and now I tell you even with tears" (Phil 3:18).

We must not forget that the Evil One in the desert offered Jesus all the powers of this world: "To you I will give their glory and all authority: for it has been given over to me, and I give it to anyone I please" (Luke 4:6).

But Jesus repelled him by choosing the way of the cross.

Through the eyes of faith, there is no other road to resurrection than the way of the cross. How could one not remember the magnificent words of Paul Evdokimov?—"Any great love is necessarily crucified."

As Olivier Clément notes:

> *Perhaps only this incomprehensible annihilation of a divine Person on the cross can convince man of God's mad love for him. The Living One, crucified,*

*becomes the God always on a lower level, hence-
forth present at depths greater than the deepest
despair of man, than his most infernal opacity.*[68]

God's madness of which St. Paul speaks (1 Corinthians 1:18-
25) is the madness of love manifested in the cross.

A New Christ?

We sometimes get the impression that the world desires another
gospel, a modified Christ, a strong-armed God. Yet God comes to
us as a feeble, poor child and as a defenseless crucified man.

Let us examine in faith and love this Jesus on the cross who the
Good Thief met in weakness and annihilation.

What kind of Church does the world want? A Church that
preaches mercy—a *fake* mercy and not the true one – a Church that
comes down from the cross and no longer preaches the shocking
nature and folly of the message, a Church that sacrifices truth in
order to attract the greatest possible number of people?

Must not the Church, on the contrary, live through the annihilation of the Crucified One before realizing the "new Pentecost of
love" proclaimed by recent Popes? God alone knows, and we must
not play prophet. Still, on Calvary, Christ's mission had "apparently" failed and the world had triumphed. The apostles had fled;
all around people were laughing derisively at the crucified Jesus.
The Good Thief, the criminal, the bandit was the only one to defend
Jesus. He alone recognized His royal nature. In fact, Christ's
royalty lies precisely here, in radical annihilation, in mockery, in
the mordant and sarcastic irony of the chief priests and the
Pharisees. In reality, the Church is only in communion with this
mystery of annihilation in the irony of the world when it dares to
proclaim the truth of salvation by the cross.

Christianity without the Cross?

Are not the poor and sinful, who acknowledge and confess their
sins, the ones who best grasp the mystery of the cross? The abyss of

their misery calls for the summit of mercy. The abyss of their sinfulness calls for the summit of grace. How many destitute, marginalized people, prisoners and ex-drug addicts understand the gospel far better than those who are learned and "righteous"?

From the moment we place our trust solely in the infinite value of the cross of Jesus Christ, as did the Good Thief, and when we ourselves are crucified with Him, we no longer belong to the "world." Only then can we become saints. The Good Thief accepted his suffering, and showed the way, the "little way" of surrender that leads to the holiness of the poor.

How many captives, wounded by life, drug addicts and alcoholics could journey rapidly to holiness if they learned to surrender their "crosses"—their emptiness and destitution— in love? For we can be freed from sin and its consequences only if we die and rise in Jesus Christ, only if we, in fact, share his cross in order to share his resurrection and receive from him the life of the new man.

Paul Preaches the Crucified Christ

Saint Paul wrote to the Corinthians: "Jews demand signs and Greeks desire wisdom, but we proclaim Christ crucified, a stumbling block to Jews and foolishness to Gentiles" (1 Corinthians 1:22-23).

God accomplished salvation not by sensational means founded on prestige and power but by *humanly unacceptable* means, by abasements, by the folly of the ignominious death of his Son on the cross.

We must read the beginning of the first letter to the Corinthians (1 Corinthians 1:17-31). Since God has chosen to save man by the folly of the cross, salvation will come to them only by preaching this folly. It will not be based on learned speeches and the specious arguments of the wise and intelligent in the eyes of the world; nor will it be based on the ostentation of powerful and prestigious means; nor on the allurements of a life of ease and comfort. On the contrary, it will be based deliberately on means that are poor and scorned and that place the emphasis on what, according to human criteria, is folly: "the gospel of the beatitudes."

Saint Paul knew that our salvation lies in Christ's cross: "God decided, through the foolishness of our proclamation, to save those who believe" (1 Corinthians 1:21).

And in conformity to what he said, Paul realized that the majority of early Christians were not learned and mighty people, but the poor, the marginalized and the weak. Through this weakness and abjection God takes pleasure in confounding the wisdom and power of the world, as he has done, in his Christ. It is therefore precisely in human weakness and suffering, as in Christ crucified, the innocent Lamb, that the power of the Spirit is manifested (cf. 1 Corinthians 1:26-29).

The Innocent Recognized by the Sinner

Jesus is the Innocent abandoned by all. He was put in the rank of criminals and he recites Psalm 22 on the cross, the Psalm of the poor par excellence. *He has come only to reveal to the world the mystery of his Father and of his merciful love. It is this weakness of Jesus that we must receive in faith if we wish to open ourselves to divine life. Christ on the cross is the Lamb of God, that is, the Innocent, Isaiah's servant, who takes upon himself the sin of the world, who grants forgiveness of sins (John 20:22-23).*

This is the time, at the very moment when the irony of the chief priests is unleashed, they who are asking for a decisive sign, that the mystery of Jesus' mercy is revealed."

While Jesus is surrounded by general mockery, the Good Thief solemnly acknowledges his innocence. [...]

In the atrocity of his torture, Jesus is aware that he is opening access to the Kingdom of forgiveness and reconciliation, to the Kingdom of divine mercy: "Today you will be ..." Then the sign of divine mercy, at the very heart of the Passion, is the repentant Good Thief who was the first to see the glory of the Risen One.

M. J. Le Guillou
L'Innocent, Cerf, 1998.

Chapter 4

The Mystery of Death and Mercy

J esus' life has passed. The end has come. Many people crossed
his path while he was here, both friends and enemies. This is his
final encounter, with a *latro*, a *criminal*, a *thief* in the broadest sense
of the word. On the threshold of death, it is a brief and final
dialogue with such a man.

> "Remember me when you come into your Kingdom,"
> says the thief.
>
> "Today you will be with me in Paradise," Jesus replies
> (Luke 23:39-41).

Hardly five seconds of conversation—very brief. But what is
said at the moment of death often contains the meaning of an entire
lifetime, and those who hear or read these words must meditate
them at length to grasp their full impact. And still, their *full impact*,
is saying a great deal!

We may think, without any risk of being mistaken, that the
"me" the Good Thief wants Jesus to remember is not the image of
his deeds but rather that it is the *"me"* he really *is*. It is the one
preserved with all of his humanity and his dignity in spite of the
criminal acts committed—*his human self which was created in the*

image of God. In his cry to Jesus, the Good Thief spontaneously exposes his dignity as a human being. But his awareness of personal dignity certainly does not go so far as to hope that the law and justice of this earth will acknowledge that dignity which lies hidden behind the criminal image shaped by his deeds. Still, this hope to have his personal dignity recognized in his body and soul has certainly led him, to a great extent, to raise his final plea to Jesus: "Remember me when you come into your Kingdom." And Jesus, without any doubt, detected a hunger and thirst for justice in the Good Thief when he replied, "Truly I tell you, today you will be with me in Paradise."

Paradise is the crowning word in the short dialogue between the Good Thief and Jesus of Nazareth. This word in the various languages of the ancient Eastern world, strictly speaking, means *garden.* It is an image of the happiness of man, and particularly of human happiness in the beginning of Creation—*paradisiacal happiness*. In the context of the Bible, it is *Eden*, the *earthly paradise.* The *Garden of Eden,* from the fall of man until now is the *lost paradise—the state of paradisiacal happiness* that no longer exists on earth.

But on the threshold of death, Jesus promises this *paradisiacal happiness* to the Good Thief. By this, he reveals to him that the *paradise is not lost* forever in the remote depths of human history, enshrouded in the fantastic stories of ancient mythologies. It lies at the end of earthly existence for all the unconsoled people of this world who open themselves to mercy; for those who have failed lamentably, for the poor and the sinners. This *paradisiacal happiness regained* is the happy fate awaiting those who experience exclusion from happiness in this world. This is Jesus' teaching on the Mount: "Happy are you who are poor, for yours is the Kingdom of God" (Luke 6:20). To understand this well one only has to read the parable of the rich man and Lazarus (Luke 16:19-31).

The rich man is not named. With all his wealth, this man has closed his heart to others and to God. By opening himself to compassion and love, he would have woven eternal bonds; but he preferred wealth to love, possessions to being, and he created an abyss of hollowness around himself. He simply did not take notice of the poor man's distress. The text does not say that he was immoral. He did not kill, he did not steal and he did not commit evil. He was not an "evil" rich man on the level of normal morality. Only that, in the midst of his festivities, he forgot one thing: he did not see the pauper at his door, nor did he did wish to take him into account.

In the parable related by Luke, the rich man who has just died complains to Abraham of his agony in the dwelling place of the dead. Meanwhile poor Lazarus, this less-than-nothing, pathetic man who spent his life begging at the rich man's gate, is happy in paradise. Jesus then has Abraham answer: "Child, remember that during your lifetime you received your good things, and Lazarus in like manner evil things; but now he is comforted here, and you are in agony" (Luke 16:25). The rich man then asks that his brothers on earth be warned of the fate awaiting them after death. Jesus concludes the parable by stating that this would be useless. For even if someone rose from the dead to warn them, the rich simply do not hope for a paradise, they already have it on earth! "Woe to you who are rich, for you have received your consolation" (Luke 6:24). This is what we call a *gospel paradox*.

The poor man has a well-defined name. *El'azar* means *God-has-helped* or *God-helps*. He represents the one who places his trust in the Lord and not in riches. According to the *Magnificat* of Mary, "The Lord fills the hungry with good things, and sends the rich away empty" (Luke 1:53). This is Jesus' mission, he is "sent to bring the good news to the poor."

The poor man, who has nothing to lean on, is open to faith and hope. Deprived of the things of the earth, he turns to the Father. He is ready to enter into the Kingdom. He thirsts for justice and places all his hope in the one who "fills the hungry with good things." Just as the rich man was not "evil," Lazarus is not filled with virtues; he is in agony, he is poor, he is thirsty. In the end, the parable justifies *El'azar*. He has placed his hope in God. He was detached and ready at any moment to enter into the Kingdom of God. He merited the first place on Abraham's bosom in the banquet of the Kingdom, just as St. John reclined on Jesus during the Last Supper (John 13:25).

As we follow the paradoxical logic of Jesus' teaching, we can also compare the Good Thief with the rich young man of the

Gospel. The Good Thief who probably broke many commandments is *assured of going to Paradise*, whereas the rich young man *who has kept all the commandments* goes away from Jesus, grieving precisely because he is rich. Jesus says about him, "It is easier for a camel to go through the eye of a needle than for someone who is rich to enter the kingdom of God" (Mt 19:24).

In the same line of thought, Jesus reveals that at *the last judgment* many "will inherit the Kingdom prepared since the foundation of the world" without ever having thought that they had a right to do so (cf. Mt 25:34-40). What will count is the good we have done or not done to the "least of these" *lowly ones* with whom Jesus identifies himself. These *lowly ones*—are *those who are hungry and thirsty, those who have neither shelter nor clothing, those who are sick or in prison.* They are all who are deprived of love and tenderness and even of natural virtue; in short all the distressed of this world, among the likes of which the Good Thief was numbered! The gospel teaching about the poor is persistent: *the Kingdom of Heaven is theirs.*

When Jesus told the Good Thief that he would be with him "today in paradise," he was not speaking in vain. The Good Thief was addressing Jesus as a *King*, as someone who possesses a *Kingdom*. He appeared to know that *Jesus' Kingdom* was not of this world ("… when you come into your Kingdom"). His own life had been such a lamentable failure and he *hoped* that Jesus would remember him when he *would come into His Kingdom.*

The dialogue between Jesus and the Good Thief therefore bears essentially on what follows physical death. Today, we either forget *the last moments of our lives* or we launch ourselves, without too much thought, into talk tinged with fantasy, often incoherent, in regard to what we call the *beyond*. We will not attempt to refute all the myths, except to say that the *imaginary realm* is still and will always be something of the *visible* and belongs to the physical world, *to the present world.* What is *invisible* is inaccessible to the body and the imagination. The *paradise* of which Jesus speaks is *invisible*; the *Kingdom* of Jesus is *invisible. Supernatural hope alone* is here below "the conviction of things not seen" (Heb 11:1), of the *invisible existence* of paradise and the Kingdom of heaven.

Paradise is not merely *nirvana*, a state of non-suffering, of apathy, that we could reach on our own at the end of a long road that would free us from pain here below and from successive reincarnations after death. Our deeds do not necessarily follow us, they do not inevitably bring on our salvation or our loss of it; there is no *karma*, anymore than *samsara*, that is *reincarnations*, other earthly lives either to do better or to sink to greater depths.

When we face death, every word becomes important. No fancy talk, only what is essential. There is no more intonation, only a breath, one last breath. It is the moment of truth. There is nothing left—neither the good life we thought we were leading, nor the bad one; not possessions, not reputation, not virtues, not malice. There is no longer enough awareness to be able to make an examination of conscience. There is only the stark naked hope—"Remember me ..." *Me*! I no longer have a name, no real importance here on earth. It is only *me, me alone* who will pass through the *eye of the needle* of death: "Oh! Remember me!" All hope is contained in this cry, the hope that is "the conviction of things not seen." And when we are convinced, no need of proof or demonstration, not even of doctrine or preaching—we have the proof, period!

The Good Thief *hopes*, for he *is convinced* that the Kingdom of Heaven exists. The one who *hopes* at the moment of death has this conviction. He has the conviction of things not seen: "... we understand that the worlds were prepared by the word of God, so that what is seen was made from things that are not visible" (Heb 11:3). This is no longer about statements but about reality itself! All that remains is to beg: "Remember me ..." for that is what is really important. This is a spontaneous call on the part of the Good Thief (he probably did not think that he was *good*, any more than that he was *evil*). He was *convinced of the existence of the Kingdom* and he cried out like the shipwrecked sailor who finally sees a boat coming toward him: "Save me!" The drowning man does not feel that he is unworthy of being saved. In that moment *he feels that he is more important than all the deeds he may have performed during his life, either good or bad*. If he had not had this hope, the Good Thief would never have called out; he would have died and simply would have been buried like the rich man of the parable (Luke 16:22).

As they watched the rich young man walk away, the astounded disciples asked Jesus, "Who then can be saved?" Jesus looked at them and said, "For mortals, it is impossible, but for God all things are possible" (Mt 19:25-26). What must we understand? Only this—no human being can save himself on his own, *God alone saves!* Acquired virtue is not what saves us, any more than the accumulated merits of our deeds. In truth, there is nothing left at the moment of death but *divine hope.*

On the threshold of death, what rose to the lips of the Good Thief, what submerged him was his recognition as a created being—a sinner who has lost paradise and who would like to return. This explains Jesus' answer that is so precise: "Today you will be with me in Paradise."

The Good Thief's deeds were not very good, and neither are ours—hence the reality that *Paradise is lost* to us, but for God! If Jesus can affirm to the Good Thief: "Today you will be with me in Paradise," it is because God has never ceased seeing "everything that he had made, and indeed, it was very good" (Gen 1:31). *Divine* hope is the *proof that God always sees his creatures as being very good* in spite of all the sins. He removes the sin of men from before his face and *sees them as He created them—very good.* In that sense, *Paradise* always exists in God, it is the "Kingdom prepared since the foundation of the world" of which Jesus speaks (Mt 25:34).

If we had to attribute a special grace for our time to the Good Thief's example, it would be that of *divine hope.* Divine hope is also the source of freedom for the *children of God* of whom "creation waits with eager longing for the revealing" (Rom 8:19). Indeed, hope, by its very nature, sets the things of this world in their *rightful place* again. Some, by *hope,* will be freed from despair and superstitions. Others will be freed from the love of money, which is "a root of all kinds of evil" (1 Tim 6:10). For all of us, *hope* will mean being freed from the spirit of fear and servitude that prevents us from crying out: "Abba! Father!" (Rom 8:15). This is how the children of God will manifest themselves.

I Call Him by His Name ...

Throughout the endlessness of their torture, a comforting intimacy established itself between Jesus and one of the criminals. It culminated in this incredible dialogue reported to us by Luke (23:42-43). This is one of the rare occasions in the gospel when someone called Jesus by his first name. Those who approached him, and even his disciples, addressed him especially as "Lord" or "Master." The Good Thief, in all his simplicity, is not embarrassed by this conventional rule. "Jesus," he said. We may think that such familiarity reveals an encounter without words, on the level of a heart already won over and transformed by the love of Christ.

Is it possible to become a saint at the last moment of one's life, in spite of a life of sinning? Yes, the Good Thief is an example of this. The Good Thief is the image of the man who is going to die. He is the only dying person whose journey to holiness through repentance and reconciliation is recorded in Holy Scripture. So we have the great advantage, as people who destined to die, to be able to follow his footsteps, to re-enact his faith in Christ, his wager on Life—and we hope to hear, in turn, when we come to our final hour, the ineffable promise from which he was the first to benefit on that Good Friday Eve.

In the office of Noon on Friday, the Catholic liturgy invites us insistently to address this confident and bold prayer to Christ the Redeemer. It deserves to be known by all:

> *Lord Jesus Christ, you who have allowed the criminal who acknowledged his sins to move from the cross to your Kingdom, we beseech you as we confess our sins: as soon as we die open for us the gates of paradise.*

What a beautiful prayer, that should be made known to those who are seriously ill, to cancer patients in their terminal phase, to the victims of AIDS and to all who are close to death. Is this not Christ's most ardent wish, that the promise he made to the Good Thief be renewed in each one of us?

Icon of the One about to Die

There are many people nowadays who die alone, in anguish, and who, because of a lack of pastoral care, have no one to prepare them to die and to accept their cross. Many do not have the opportunity to receive the sacraments. Who will speak to them of mercy, who will dare to give them hope by speaking to them of the example of the Good Thief?

At a time when all kinds of pressures are exercised to legalize euthanasia and when so many questions about death remain unanswered for, it is more urgent than ever to look to the agonizing saint of Golgotha.

At the moment of our death, our situation will be rigorously identical with his: "We are hung on the cross with Christ and similar in his death."[69]

Like that of the Good Thief, our crosses can be united to the cross of Jesus who, during his agony, sees us as he saw his companion in torture, hears us as he heard him, forgives us as he forgave him. He sanctifies us as he sanctified him if we allow him as he did, to purify, transform and recreate us by his merciful love.

Indeed, where can we find a clearer and sounder or more invigorating answer, or more *hope* filled, in response to our questions about death than in Jesus' promise to the Good Thief? As St. Ambrose said in words that resound in the Church: "Life consists in being with Christ: wherever Christ is, there is the Kingdom!"

Moreover, if we hope to benefit personally from the Good Thief's example and, to die as he did, how could we not desire a celebration that would commemorate him in our churches and chapels, and welcomed in the liturgical calendar? Why not have celebrations in honor of the holy Good Thief, especially on 12 October, since that is the day on which he figures in the Jerusalem calendar?

The Good Thief, Patron Saint of a Holy Death?

The Good Thief represents a model of authentic and universal holiness, which is addressed primarily to the men and women for whom the trial of the cross is associated, consciously or not, with the Passion and death of Christ—all who are forsaken, rejected or judged. He is also a model for those who have been away from the Church for twenty, thirty or forty years, and who are afraid of being condemned—who do not dare believe in the possibility of being forgiven by God. Is not the Good Thief also a model for AIDS victims who are abandoned, sometimes even by their family, and who die in an appalling solitude, crucified in the eyes of the world?

What words of hope there are in the gospel of the Good Thief! The merciful Christ, present at the agony of the Good Thief, remains close to us when we in our turn are on the cross. We all have the possibility of reliving the story of the Good Thief and of proclaiming Christ's divine mercy through our death.

That is why many voices are rising and asking that, along with St. Joseph, the holy Good Thief be named as the patron saint of a "holy death." Could we doubt for a single moment that the dying would identify with him in great brotherly love?

For all those whose conscience is "heavy" and who do not dare to believe in the forgiveness and mercy of God—whose witness speaks more clearly than that of the "thief of paradise," as Thérèse of Lisieux calls him?

For those who ask, the grace of a holy death experienced by The Good Thief cannot be refused.

Marthe Robin said:

> *Between the apparent and the real death, there is always a moment, the one when God offers his mercy and his divine forgiveness. But man always remains free ...*

St. Catherine of Siena declared that what would decide the fate of every man, would be *the final act of trust he would make or refuse to make.* She said that at the last moment God would grant to every man a grace that would reveal to him the possibility of making an act of total trust in him.

I believe that at the moment of death, grace performs deeds in hearts that are akin to a miracle.

When God visits his [created] children in the final agonizing hand to hand struggle; or in the abyss between the clinical and real death—it in this moment that he alone knows the secret of Gethsemane and the descent into hell and he places freedom on the edge of an inexpressible beatitude.[70]

Would this not be the Good Thief's hour, the hour of hope in God's infinite mercy? Wonders may happen at the last moment of our lives. To return to a quotation from a great theologian, Cardinal Charles Journet:

> *I believe that miraculous conversions are very numerous and that, because of the prayers of God's saints and friends, many great sinners are converted at the last moment of their lives ... Human beings who will have lived far from God, will, at the very last moment, be able to turn to God without our knowing anything about it.*[71]

I recall a man who confided to me that after meditating on the Good Thief and praying for a non-baptized member of his family who described herself as an agnostic, he had the joy of seeing this person suddenly touched by grace on her deathbed. She asked for baptism and she died like the Good Thief—like a saint.

Do we think of the Good Thief and pray for those who are dying, even for those who seem to have rejected both God and the faith for a long time? Do we not lack hope and faith? Do we not know that *accepting* the merciful Love who is offering himself may be enough to be saved and sanctified at the last moment since God is the one who saves *through grace*?

> And love can save a man even at the last second of a bad life—if, in that second, the man has found the light of love—perhaps if he has always believed that

God is love.[72] The Good Thief is the saint of "the last moment" when God is able to mend a whole life. We must ask God with faith for the grace of a good death, and not only of a good death but also of a *holy* death, and this grace of graces of entering paradise in an instant as he did.

"The fire of love is more sanctifying than that of purgatory," said Thérèse of Lisieux and, she added, "I want to appear before God, like the Good Thief, with empty hands."

The Good Thief, patron saint of a holy death for us, poor sinners that we are. Perhaps he has a role to play, complementary to that of St. Joseph, especially for great sinners agonizing in death, so that they may not yield to despair and but have the grace of repentance.

Making Our Death a Hymn to Mercy

Death comes at the end of our days "that pass away like smoke" (Ps 102:3), that "are like a passing shadow" (Ps 144:4). Death is unavoidable and universal. "For our allotted time is like the passing of a shadow, and there is no return from death, because it is sealed up and no one turns back" (Wisdom 2:5).

"Our outer nature is wasting away" (2 Corinthians 4:16) and "the present form of this world is passing away" (1 Corinthians 7:31).

"There is for all one entrance into life, and one way out" (Wisdom 7:6). No one knows the hour of his death. Man, like beast, is from dust and will return to dust. This is the language we hear constantly.

Death comprises physical, moral, emotional and spiritual suffering all at the same time. Before death, we must face the same questions. It is a tragedy, a failure, degeneration.[73]

But death is not annihilation. It is a "falling into sleep." It is the anticipation of a mystery to be deciphered, a return of our being into the holiness of God.[74]

Christ alone holds the key to death. He accepted his own death. After the anguish and the sweat of blood, he went out to meet it, freely: "No one takes my life, I give it freely myself." He offered his death. He experienced it intensely.

He, who was present during the agony of his companion in crucifixion, is now present for us when we, in turn, are on our cross. Therefore we are never alone. We are offered the possibility to live out, in our turn, the story of the Good Thief and to make of our own death a hymn to divine mercy.

We, in our death are united to that of Christ, and can make a gift, an offering, a hymn of love and trust, a liturgy ...

Thérèse said, "I am not dying, I am entering into Life!" From that moment, death is not an end, but the beginning of our future.

With Christ, we have already passed from death to life, to eternal life:

> *Therefore we have been buried with him by baptism into death, so that, just as Christ was raised from the dead by the glory of the Father, we too might walk in the newness of life. For if we have been united with him in a death like his, we will certainly be united with him in a resurrection like his. We know that our old self was crucified with him so that the body of sin might be destroyed, and we might no longer be enslaved to sin. For whoever has died is freed from sin (Rom 6:4-7)*

In death we can become like Christ:

> *I want to know Christ and the power of his resurrection and the sharing of his sufferings by becoming like him in death" (Phil 3:10).*

> *"I have been crucified with Christ; and it is no longer I who live, but it is Christ who lives in me (Gal 2:19-20).*

Living in Christ by dying with him, like the Good Thief; the two dying together in order to live eternally in face-to-face encounter. For now we see in a mirror dimly, but then we will see face to face. Now I know only in part; then I will know fully, even as I have been fully known (1 Corinthians 13:12).

The Good Thief is the saint of the end times and of our final moments.

Is not our silence about him the consequence of the Pharisaic idea we have of God? It is true that the persona of the Good Thief is at the opposite pole of our mentality regarding honest people. It upsets the narrow views we have of the mystery of redemption. Man exalts riches, the Thief embodies total poverty.

To testify to his infinite mercy, the redeeming Christ chooses a "well of iniquity," an "ember from hell," as the Fathers of the Church said. He chooses it and he canonizes it! This man lacking everything, whom human justice has nailed to the wood of infamy and woe, is the one chosen by the crucified Jesus Christ as "the firstborn of the elect"!

Yes, life is mightier than death! "Where, O death is your sting?" (1 Corinthians 15:55).

Obscuring the Good Thief deprives the thousands of men, women and children who are dying each day of an example of conversion *in extremis.* His is a witness able to ignite in them—when the darkness of death, often terrifying, comes upon them—*the supreme hope in Love that forgives.* A multitude of suffering beings nailed to implacable crosses are struggling painfully in the stifling darkness of a mechanical and heartless world. Their cries rend the universe! Do we hear them? They are awaiting an ultimate reason to hope, they are awaiting an image of the saved where they might recognize themselves. They are waiting for someone of their own to come and to tell them, "Why do you despair when I have hoped? For nothing is impossible by God's infinite mercy!"

May we not close the doors of our hearts against the cry of the crucified Jesus calling for humanity to come and slake its thirst at the inexhaustible source springing from his Heart!

O folly of the uncreated Wisdom, which finds pleasure in making its power burst forth by saving man from the most desperate situations! How could we not lose ourselves in the meditation of this mysterious plan of mercy? More than anywhere else, is this not where we will be able to rediscover a childlike soul and a pauper's heart? In a word: the salt of the gospel!

The gospel episode of the Good Thief upsets our hierarchy of values. God has no need of our titles of glory; he needs only our empty hands. And all that is fulfilled in the supreme moment of Christ's Passover, in nearness and likeness to the crucified Savior, the true incarnation of the mystery of mercy!

It becomes urgent for us to give our attention to this ultimate witness of the infinite mercy of the crucified Jesus Christ. This mercy was manifested through him on Good Friday and it still manifests itself today in all those who open themselves to it, filled with invincible hope in the One who let himself be crucified by love.

Each expression of the Word bears the burden of eternity; Jesus' words to the Good Thief were uttered for our salvation, and Christ reinforced these with a solemn oath: "Truly I tell you," so that his mercy for repentant sinners may be manifested to the entire world.

Would not relegating the immense impact of this great gospel fact to the shadows, be an insult to the Word of God? If the Good Thief's example is not important for the Church and for the world; if his example of repentance and true penance is not addressed to everyone—would the evangelist have included the story in the gospel?

We can glorify God by our death, as did the Good Thief. It may even become "a supreme apostolate,"[75] for:

> ... *Indeed, we do not live to ourselves, and we do not die to ourselves. If we live, we live to the Lord, and if we die, we die to the Lord; so then, whether we live or whether we die, we are the Lord's (Rom 14:7-8).*

With the Good Thief, we can sing, "I shall not die, but I shall live, and recount the deeds of the Lord!" (Ps 118:17).

A concluding quotation is drawn from Romano Guardini's book *Les Fins dernières:*

> *Death is the final act of human life; but in every life this act is essential. This final end of human life determines everything that preceded it. As the proverb says, "All's well that ends well." In the current sense, that amounts to saying: "If the end is a success, even barely so, the whole itself is in some way justified. In its deep sense: if the end turns out good, it is because of the dynamism of the whole, and in an honest end; the all is "perfected," receives its definitive worth. Only the final notes of a melody confer upon it its total presence, only the outcome of a play sets the hero's personality in full light: this is how death leads man's life to its fulfillment.*[76]

Losing All Is Gaining All

It is in his death that Jesus descended into hell and in death itself he is glorified. It is there that he meets all people in their deaths, and enables them to die together with him as he goes to the Father. To join with him in his resurrection, it is necessary to be able to die with him, in order to rise with him.

Death is a decisive stage in the fulfillment of every man. What happens in death? Catholic tradition speaks of a particular judgment that Christ exercises at the moment of death. It is proper however to rectify the notion of divine justice as it is anchored in many minds. God exercises his justice not by punishing but by communicating his justice, that is, his holiness, to the one who opens himself to it. We must say this: divine justice is exercised in every man who accepts the justice that is in the risen Christ (Rom 3:23-26) for our own justification (Rom 4:25).

Let the heart that fears death, then, be reassured! Christ will come to meet each one of us in our death by a calling presence. Jesus promised: 'Those who hate their life (who accept to die by abandoning themselves) will keep it for eternal life, and where I am there will my servant be also' (John 12:25 ff.). Ignatius of Antioch longed for a death that would plunge him into Christ. Death is the encounter with Christ. Christians of the early Church thought of men before Christ; but most of the men today still belong to the period before Jesus Christ, they do not know him. The gospel does not reach them, they do not encounter Christ during their life on earth, and therefore, they cannot give him their faith.

"Now, Jesus would not have died for all if at least in their death he did not offer himself to all so that they may be united to him, in his saving death.

"Since Jesus came for sinners (Luke 5:32), man at the moment of his death must surrender himself into the hands of the Father and abandon himself to the immensity of the Love of God offering itself. Death is Christian when it accepts a total loss. But to lose all is to gain all, for it is impossible for us to give everything without receiving everything. To die of love is the greatest blessedness."

François-Xavier Durrwell
Christ, Humankind and Death, Mediaspaul

Chapter 5

A Model of True Holiness

Each of us is called to become holy. Vatican II also reminds us of that (*LG* 45). The call to holiness, however, is incomprehensible to those who have a wrong notion of what holiness is.

Holiness is not a product of our good dispositions, or our natural generosity, or our supposed virtues. To think that we can sanctify ourselves through great deeds, even apostolic acts, and attribute merit through these to ourselves would simply be prideful. We must never forget this—this is a fundamental basis of Christian faith, especially as articulated by St. Paul. In the supernatural order, we are absolutely unable to attain holiness on our own efforts, or through our techniques or methods. Everything is the result of the pure "gift" of God's grace that we can only receive as beggars. St. Augustine had this idea adopted by the Council of Carthage during the fourth century, to counter the heresy of Pelagius who upheld the notion that, on our own and without grace, we would be able to attain some good in our journey to salvation. The heresy of Pelagianism is the belief—unconsciously most of the time—that we can achieve holiness through our own efforts.

Speaking of semi-Pelagianism, Cardinal Danneels declared:

> *[It is] all that is totally anti-Christian and anti-evangelistic. And this is the real tragedy of the Church*

today: the denial of the dogma of the absolute neces-
sity of grace. We would need a new but slightly
modified St. Augustine. He is the one who, in the
beginning, rescued the Church from the great temp-
tation of practically denying Jesus' declaration:
"Without me, you can do nothing."[77]

Often, holiness is confused with external perfection and natural
virtue. As Bossuet said concerning the Jansenist nuns of Port-
Royal, who projected an image of fortitude and heroism in the practice of virtues: "Yes, they are virtuous like angels, but proud like
demons."

True holiness is not necessarily identified with virtue. God does
not want righteous people who have justified themselves by their
own actions. Neither is holiness moral perfection. We can prove
that we possess relative human perfection simply by the fact that we
are endowed with a fine heredity, strength of character, a good
family heritage, and still be a long way from holiness.

Elisabeth of the Trinity said:

It seems to me that the guiltiest soul is the one who is
most justified in hoping. This act of forgetting
herself and throwing herself into the arms of God
glorifies him and gives him more joy than all these
concentrations on herself and all these examinations
that make her live with her infirmities.

And the theologian Hans Urs von Balthasar commented:

It is not by gazing on our woes that we will be
purified, but by casting our eyes on the One who is
all purity and holiness.
The presence of the Redeemer and of Redemption
through him, and the purification of the soul requires
only that a simple gaze be turned to him. By this act
of self-forgetfulness, the soul receives the forgiveness

of sins. This act makes her acknowledge her sin and divine grace.[78]

Often we tend to think that holiness is acquired through our merits or our works, and we overlook the almighty power of grace. In reality, God is the one who makes us saints [holy]; it is the freely-given love of Christ, freely accepted by us, that recreates us and transforms us in an instant, thus making us able to love, as Christ did. For the Good Thief, this was very brief, for others, it will be longer. The laborers of the last hour received the same reward as those of the first—a reality that annoyed the latter.

Thérèse of Lisieux understood this very well. We have but to read over her Act of Consecration to the merciful Love of 9 June 1895, or this declaration of the *Novissima verba*: "I have no works ... ah well! He will deal with me according to his own works."

There is a link between misery and mercy. If holiness involves dying to self, is not the experience of our weakness and the loving acceptance of it the radical means of leading us to this death?

Such is the lesson given to us in the Good Thief. All he has is his poverty, the acceptance of his misery, the avowal of his state as a sinner; he has obviously totally given up the quest for his own grandeur.

As F. X. Durrwell stated:

> *The saints instinctively felt how close their weakness as sinners was to the sanctifying power of God: "O God, I am happy to feel small and weak in your sight, and my heart is at peace in joy," said Thérèse of Lisieux.*[79]

It must be stated clearly—whoever reduces Christianity to good morality empties it of everything that gives it meaning. Several years ago Cardinal Daniélou declared:

> *After all, if it is good advice we want, Buddha gave excellent advice. People say that Christianity is*

summed up in love of our neighbor. But men did not have to wait for Christianity to love their neighbors. Claiming to have the monopoly of love for our neighbors would be thinking as the Pharisees did. There is love of one's neighbor among Buddhists; there is love of neighbors in all religions. Consequently this is not what constitutes Christianity. What does constitute Christianity is to confess that we do not love our neighbor, and because we don't love our neighbor we know that we need to be set free from those powers of evil. And this is precisely the need which is specifically met by the salvation, the redemption, given by Christ: our need to be saved from evil, because we know very well from our experience that by ourselves we are unable to conquer the evil, to conquer it in ourselves and to conquer it in others. I mean that, ultimately, faith is the essential thing.[80]*

The Good Thief also answers the errors of the New Age, as well as any claim that we can "perfect" ourselves by means of our inner strengths. He also answers the temptation portrayed in the beginning of Genesis—of "wanting to become God" on our own.

The Good Thief suggests that we go back to the gospel holiness, where God opens the doors of His Kingdom to the poorest, to the weakest, and to the most hurting.

The Epiphany of Mercy

The luminous divine message emanating from the episode of the Good Thief is that the mercy of God is without limit and absolutely freely given. It is of an almighty efficacy if we believe in it and let Him act. Without excluding anyone, it offers itself without delay, waiting only (O divine impatience of an infinitely patient God!) for us to let it be poured. To those who believe, it gives birth to a boundless hope, to an extraordinarily bold hope; allowing the greatest sufferings to be borne with fortitude and patience.

The whole Christian revelation comes down to this message. It is the heart of the gospel. The core of Christian faith consists in this: God is love. And because all men are wayward and sinners, divine love becomes tenderness and mercy for each and all.

However, we allowed the one whom Christ canonized during His sacrifice of the cross on Good Friday to fall into oblivion. Is this not an affront to his mercy? Can our poor human vision of things oppose to the counsel of wisdom? Would the one whom Christ chose as a companion in eternity be unworthy of our attention?

The Good Thief, an Example for Our Time

Pope John Paul II said:

> *To acknowledge one's sin, indeed— penetrating still more deeply into the consideration of one's own personhood – to recognize oneself as being a sinner, capable of sin and inclined to commit sin, is the essential first step in returning to God. For example, this is the experience of David, who "having done what is evil in the eyes of the Lord" and having been rebuked by the prophet Nathan, exclaims: "For I know my transgressions and my sin is ever before me. Against you, you alone, have I sinned and done what is evil in your sight." ... In the concrete circumstances of sinful humanity, there can be no conversion without the acknowledgement of one's own sin.*[81]

The Good Thief admitted he was a sinner. He saw his crucifixion as the sentence he deserved because of the crimes he had committed. What humility! "We have been condemned justly," he said. He did not try to justify himself. He did not say: "You understand, with my wounds, it is normal for me to have acted in this way." Or still: "Even if I became a thief, I only followed my conscience. Why should I be condemned for the life I led?" He did not lay the blame on society or on the environment. No, the Good Thief did not reason in this way. Inspired by the Holy Spirit, he simply admitted that he was a sinner.

When he saw the crucified Jesus, he understood his guilt; he was convinced that Jesus was innocent, that he was the total weakness of love. The Good Thief became holy because his sins were forgiven, and because he gave up justifying himself by any means.

God exercises justice by being merciful! This is the great revelation! God justifies whoever admits his sin and opens his heart to Jesus the Savior.

When St. Paul uses the word "justice," he does not use it to evoke chastisement, but rather that God's justice is the act by which God makes man just. The Apostle himself explains his conception of the "justice of God":

> *When the goodness and loving kindness of God our Savior appeared, he saved us, not because of any works of righteousness that we had done, but according to his mercy, through the water of rebirth and renewed by the Holy Spirit (Titus 3:4-5).*

To say: "God's justice has manifested itself" amounts to saying: "God's goodness, his love, his mercy have been manifested."

Since God is always "the one who is first to love" and who is first *to justify*, man must then always be the one who believes and who allows himself be justified freely. The Good Thief only hoped for grace, because he had nothing worthwhile to present to the Saviour; he could only receive everything from Jesus' cross. The Good Thief's "little way" of spiritual poverty must make us like beggars who, possessing nothing, expect everything from the pure generosity of Christ the Redeemer—our only hope.

A Church Father of the fourth century wrote the following words that are extraordinarily applicable to our times:

> *For each man, life begins from the moment when Christ was sacrificed for him. But Christ is sacri-*

*ficed for him at the very moment when he acknowl-
edges grace and becomes aware of the life that this
sacrifice has given him.*

Like the Good Thief that *moment,* if we so desire, may be *now.*
We, too, after sincere confession, may go back home *justified* just
as the publican in the temple was (cf. Luke 18:14). It was enough
for him to admit his sins and to say in all sincerity: "O my God,
have mercy on the sinner that I am."

The first step of the Holy Spirit's work in a man's heart consists
of convincing him that he is a sinner in need of a Saviour so that he
may receive salvation through the crucified and risen Jesus.

If we were not sinners, we would not need to be saved. Jesus
would not have had to die for us. Confessing our sin places us on
the way of salvation. Like the holy Good Thief, we must admit: "He
has done nothing wrong," for the more we know God's holiness, the
more we realize the depths of sin in us.

The Good Thief, through the light that could only come from
the Holy Spirit, recognized in his innermost self that the death of
Christ was for *him,* the sinner, and this hope filled him and enabled
him to believe in salvation by the cross.

The Good Thief experienced "justification." He believed that
the Lord Jesus, who is without sin, was dying on the cross for
him—bearing in his body the punishment for his own sin.

The Good Thief's Prayer

Not only did the Good Thief believe in the saving
death of Jesus, but he also voiced a sincere prayer:
"Jesus, remember me when you come into your
Kingdom" (Luke 23:42). St. Paul's letter to the
Romans echoes this prayer when he says, "Everyone
who calls on the name of the Lord shall be saved"
(Rom 10:13). Having confessed his sin and invoking
Christ, he was saved, transformed and sanctified.

The example of the Good Thief's humility is overwhelming. He says: "Remember me." No doubt he thought that a sinner, a miserable and unworthy man like him, could not claim salvation. Yet hope for mercy fills his being—if Jesus would kindly remember him, everything would then be possible.

He uttered a prayer that was certainly not perfect, but it came from a childlike heart. Jesus' answer was clear. The Good Thief's prayer was both heard and fulfilled beyond all measure: "Truly I tell you, today you will be with me in Paradise" (Luke 23:43). St. Luke places the term "today" in evidence. This term, in Luke, always expresses *the actuality of Jesus' coming as a Saviour* (cf. Luke 2:11; 4:21; 19:5-9). In response to the Good Thief, however, Jesus adds "with me" revealing to the man his condition as a disciple.

The Cross, Source of Holiness

The Good Thief shows us what the cross of Christ, the folly and wisdom of God, can accomplish. How can we possibly despair and still fear as we watch the Good Thief? If we admit we are sinners in need of salvation, then our life as Christians who contemplate the crucified Christ in faith, will become a perpetual *Magnificat*, a hymn of gratitude and hope.

Anyone, who acknowledges that he is a sinner and *confesses* his sin, even if he has committed the most degrading deeds, can be transformed into a *saint* like the Good Thief if he asks for forgiveness from the depths of his heart. For the greatest crime is nothing before the infinite holiness of Christ, our Redeemer; and the greatest criminal, who has become a repentant sinner, can indeed become a saint if he entrusts his sins to God's mercy and surrenders himself completely to His merciful love.

The Saviour of Sinners

The gospel is the Good News of mercy for the poor and for sinners who acknowledge themselves as such. In Luke's gospel Jesus, until his death, is portrayed as the Saviour of sinners. Everything he says in parables about those who are or were lost, the merciful welcome he gives to Zacchaeus—all that, so to speak, is crowned by the promise of salvation made to the Good Thief in his final hour.

What great hope we find in the fact that the Good Thief is *justified* in one instant by Jesus himself! The repentant Good Thief really becomes a *saint* and will be with Jesus in paradise, for to be "with him" is to be in paradise. St. Paul says: "My desire is to ... be with Christ" (Phil 1:23); ah well! The Good Thief will also be there *before* St. Paul. He is therefore the saint of the infinite mercy and a model for us, poor sinners.

Blessed Are Those Who Are Aware of Their Sin

Our modern world does not want to hear about sin. Some Christians say that sin is too negative and, since the gospel is Good News, we must not talk about sin. Arnold Uleyn, in his masterly work *L'Actualité de la fonction prophétique*, clearly answers this argument:

> *It is obviously and absolutely exact to define the role of the preacher of faith and the gospel as consisting in bringing the good news. But, in fact, the great question here is the following: Are the men to whom you are speaking in search for good news? Are there any people interested in this affair? It simply appears that if the good news does not reach its destination, it is because no one wants to be freed from his miserable situation. The offer is there, but there is no demand for it. And for lack of interested people, no one finds grace. Only the one who is aware of living in a state of servitude may be freed and liberated. Only the one who is aware of his need for forgiveness is disposed to accept with feelings of relief and gratitude the reconciliation offered to him. Could it not be that many in no way desire the remission of their sins for the simple reason that they absolutely do not want to acknowledge them?*[82]

To acknowledge honestly and without excuse that we have sinned is the absolute requirement, the condition to obtain forgiveness from God.

The book of Proverbs says:

> *"No one who conceals transgressions will prosper,*
> *but the one who confesses and forsakes them will*
> *obtain mercy" (Proverbs 28:13).*

Psalm 32 expresses this thought still more clearly:

> *While I kept silence, my body wasted away through*
> *my groaning all day long ... Then I acknowledged*
> *my sin to you, and I did not hide my iniquity; I said,*
> *"I will confess my transgressions to the Lord" and*
> *you forgave the guilt of my sin (32:3, 5).*

When acknowledging his own guilt and God's justice, the sinner ceases protesting against his fate. He gives glory to God and entrusts himself entirely to his mercy, as the Good Thief did.

The Good Thief's Holiness

The example of the Good Thief presents us with a model of authentic and universal holiness.

But two questions come to mind:

1.   What did the Good Thief do to become a saint in such a short time?

Everything began with two gazes that met. First, Jesus' compassionate gaze stirred respect and sympathy in the Good Thief's heart. Then, within the endless moments of suffering, a true friendship, an intimacy, a bond made him cross, in an instant, every phase of a penitent reconciliation—acknowledgement and confession of his wrong deeds, faith in God's mercy, contrition, atonement, request for and acceptance of Christ's forgiveness, testimony and sharing.

2. Why does Jesus canonize this man who, until then, has only committed misdeeds rather than canonizing a just and honest man whose past is filled with merit and good deeds?

We are in awe before Jesus' extraordinary psychology and the exquisitely delicate movement of his heart. Let us imagine for a moment what would have taken place if he had chosen and canonized a fine man, a victim of partisan passion as he himself was. We would have explained this very naturally as the canonization of the holiness and the works of a righteous man. We would not have had this shining and invigorating evidence where Christ, with unparalleled brilliance, reveals the unfathomable mercy of God. We would have ignored the fact that God chooses weakness to confound power, and thus we would have continued to judge the immeasurable greatness of grace according to our own scale of values.

In the Old Testament book of Leviticus we see God's commandment: "You shall be holy, for I the Lord your God am holy" (Leviticus 19:2). But how can we respond to this? By putting into practice the two poles, the two facets, the two gems of this commandment: "You shall love the Lord your God with all your heart, and with all your soul, and with all your might" (Deuteronomy 6:5), and: "You shall love your neighbor as yourself" (Leviticus 19:18).

Jesus, in turn, reminds us of this requirement. We have forgotten it, leaving it up to the spiritually elite to respond and, as for ourselves, we remain content with being as we are.

The message presented by the Good Thief is that love, does not impose itself. There can be no love unless there is freedom. Because we are free, we can accept God's gift of himself to us just as we can also refuse it.

The other thief, who was in the same situation and had the same freedom, did not accept the grace offered to him, at least from what we know of the account in the gospels.

The story of the Good Thief places their roles exactly within the work of holiness: Christ is the first actor. His love freely accepted transforms or re-creates us. Personal "merit" then grows as time is given to us, because when we love, we conform ourselves to the will of the one we love.

Finally the Good Thief enables us to understand that holiness can economize on time precisely because it is dependent on love and that "love," Thérèse tells us, "does not need time to accomplish its work in a soul."

What an adorable pedagogy of Jesus' tenderness! He chooses a criminal with a heavily burdened past to show us clearly that his love that does everything in us as soon as we surrender ourselves to him in an act of faith—as we are and wherever we are! This is simple! Everything is in the trusting surrender of ourselves to the merciful love of Christ who invites us to choose the way traced by his companion in crucifixion.

The Theological Virtues

The grace of justification that Christ granted the Good Thief, through his Passion on the cross, blessed him with the three theological virtues: faith, hope and charity.

1.   The Heroic Faith of the Good Thief

The faith of the Good Thief, a response to the love of God, was born in his encounter with Jesus. He marked him with the seal of his Spirit so that he would become His witness.

Church Fathers have described the faith of Jesus' companion in the crucifixion as "heroic." St. John Chrysostom sums up very well the common opinion of the Church Fathers on this subject when he declares that his faith was greater "than that of the patriarchs and the prophets, than that of Abraham and Moses, than that of Isaiah and Ezekiel ..." He confessed Christ on the cross when he saw him in ignominy, whereas they, as well as the apostles and martyrs, believed in him and bound themselves to him because they had seen him in the light of his glory and of the performance of his miracles.

All the Church Fathers expressed their amazement at seeing the Good Thief confessing his faith in Christ publicly and binding himself to Jesus in spite of everything that could have dissuaded him from doing so. He knew Jesus in his rejection by the religious and political authorities as well as by the people—this general skepticism being a result of the apparent failure of his mission—and, finally, in his igno-minious death on a cross.

Thanks to Luke's gospel, the Good Thief proclaims his faith before all the nations of the earth until the end of time.

His faith was a grace, a gift of God, a supernatural virtue, but also an act of intelligence and will, both cooperating with divine grace. The Good Thief adhered personally, freely, to the truth that God was revealing to him.

Abandoned by all, scorned, rejected, condemned to an infa-mous death, he placed his whole faith in Christ, he believed in his promise. Finally, he accomplished his act of faith in prayer.

2.   **His Hope**

It lay totally in Christ.

Anchor of the soul (Heb 6:19), protection in the spiritual combat (1 Thessalonians 5:8), a motive of joy even and especially in trials (Rom 12:12), hope will not have disap-pointed him (Rom 5:5).

Through hope, a theological virtue that springs from and ends in God, the Good Thief, after hearing Jesus' promise, freed his heart from all things. No longer hoping for anything the world could offer him, he lived only in trusting anticipation of the beatific vision and a desire to be in the Kingdom proclaimed by Jesus. During the long hours of his agony, he was so deprived of human support that he raised his eyes only to the one who, at his side, had declared one day: "And I, when I am lifted up from the earth, will draw all people to myself (John 12:32).

The Good Thief "hoped against all hope" (Rom 4:18) that he would join Christ beyond death. God poured the Holy Spirit into his heart, thanks to whom he could await the return of Christ, he who "will come to be glorified by his saints and to be marveled at on that day among all who have believed" (2 Thessalonians 1:10).

So must we repeat along with St. Ambrose: "No one may judge himself as excluded from God's mercy when the Good Thief has been accepted."

3.   His Charity

Faith acts through charity, the bond of perfection, the soul of holiness and apostolate.

Charity is a theological virtue, the fruit of the Holy Spirit, and is the queen of virtues.

We can apply this text from *The Catechism of the Catholic Church* to the Good Thief:

He who believes in Christ becomes a son of God. This filial adoption transforms him ... In union with his Saviour; the disciple attains the perfection of charity, which is holiness (n° 1709).

We may note how the Church Fathers and the doctors of the Church insist on conferring the title of "martyr" on the

Good Thief. This is because of the testimony he made to the Truth at a time when it seemed almost abandoned by all (still more so today). He was baptized in his own blood, and the death he endured in a spirit of faith and charity, led him to eternal bliss immediately after his death, as Jesus had promised him.

The Gifts of the Holy Spirit and Moral Virtues

The Good Thief was able to truly live the theological virtues thanks to the gifts of the Holy Spirit, among which are fear and fortitude; and thanks to certain moral virtues, particularly justice and humility.

1. **Fear**

While on the cross, the Good Thief rebuked his companion saying: "Do you not fear God, since you are under the same sentence of condemnation?" (Luke 23:40).

This is not a servile fear, the kind of fear experienced by the slave before his master. According to its use in the Bible, this term means the profound reverence we have for the mystery of God and everything evoked by his name.

Astonishment almost always precedes fear. We sense in Luke's account that the Good Thief was struck with astonishment in the face of Jesus' behaviour, by the forgiveness he begs from his Father for those who accused him—his judges, his executioners and the multitude who decried him. In Jesus' presence, he was filled with the feeling of his unparalleled holiness. So he asked his companion to keep a certain distance—as a mark of respect—between God, whose presence he felt in this "Righteous man" who was suffering and agonizing so close to them, the criminals that they were. And at the same time, through this rebuke he seeks, as it were, closer proximity with God: "And we indeed have been condemned justly, for we are getting what we deserve for our deeds, but this man has done nothing wrong" (Luke 23:41).

The Good Thief was honest enough not to confuse their situation with that of Jesus. They are guilty while he is innocent. They knew very well the risks they were taking should they be caught, the punishment which the crimes and the violations of the law they were committing would expose them to; but he, in no way, deserved to be put in the same rank as they were.

2.   Fortitude

Such behavior also required the gift of "fortitude."

The Good Thief had nothing he could use to justify himself and still, Jesus Christ marked him with his Spirit by vesting him with fortitude from on high so that he would be his witness.

He proved his fortitude by refusing to yield either to violence or to cowardice, another form of violence, which are the exact opposites of fortitude.

The Good Thief's courage verged on boldness and revealed that holiness has nothing to do with temperament. The religious dignitaries who had claimed and obtained Jesus' sentence to death, hurled abuse at him and challenged him. Ironically, they urged him to come down from the cross, so that they might "believe." However it was in the presence of these haughty and hateful characters that the Good Thief undertook to defend Jesus and proclaim his innocence.

Fortitude of the Spirit enabled him to overcome fear and to confront the prevailing forces of opposition on that day. It disposed him to reach the stage of self-denial and sacrifice to defend Christ's just cause. The gift of the Spirit, and especially that of fortitude, made him compassionate towards Jesus.

An Example of Humility

To tell the truth about oneself, to acknowledge one's sins and admit them publicly requires great humility. The Good Thief fulfilled the condition to enter the Kingdom: he humbled himself (Matthew 23:12); he became "childlike" (Matthew 18:3-4), lowly. Because he was humble, he could testify to the truth (John 18:37), and from his cross he continued to present Christ to the poor. Because he humbled himself, he, too, was exalted (Luke 18:9-14).

He received the gift of humility, the very foundation of prayer, a grace, and a Covenant relationship established by God in the depths of our hearts. Humility and trust put him in communion with God, Christ and others.

Canonized by Jesus

On 16 November 1988, Pope John Paul II did not hesitate to use the term "saint" and the expression "the first canonization in history" in referring to the Good Thief.

Jesus promised paradise to the repentant and converted criminal on that very day. This is therefore an integral forgiveness: the one who had committed crimes and robberies—therefore sins—became a saint in the last moment of his life. We could say that this text from Luke registers the first canonization in history realized by Jesus himself ...

And the Holy Father highlighted the importance he gave to these declarations by noting at the beginning of his speech:

> *Everything Jesus taught and did during his life on earth attains the summit of truth and holiness on the cross. The words Jesus pronounces then constitute his supreme and definitive message.*[83]

Jesus' words, "Truly I tell you, today you will be with me in Paradise" (Luke 23:43) are a solemn declaration ("Truly I tell you"), like a statement pronounced *ex cathedra* from the height of the pulpit of the crucified Messiah, of the Head of the Church that will be born from his open side.[84]

In his book *Dismas, le Bon Larron*, Fr. Albert Bessières rightly wondered:

> *Was it in vain or for secondary motives that God, at the most solemn moment of the history of the world, that of the Passion, exalted this great figure, placed this penitent thief, this apostle, on the right side of Christ, at the summit of Calvary, to be the one first introduced in heaven in the footsteps of the Redeemer, on the evening of Good Friday? No, there is no need for a Christian to indulge in long reflections to see this as a great providential plan.*[85]

In his *Lettre au Bon Larron, premier client du paradis* (Letter to the Good Thief, first client of paradise), Cardinal Roger Etchegaray wrote on 19 March 1978:

> *Who could invent such words, beyond all expectations, pronounced in a solemn and friendly tone in a calm assurance? Those words forbid us ever to lose hope about anyone ... The word of God is always effective in creation. The love of God hastens us through the stages we believe we ought to follow. In an instant, the abyss is crossed and Redemption is made even more wonderful than creation.*

The example of the one who attended the sacrifice of Christ on the cross, who was associated with his redeeming sufferings, who received from his lips the promise of the eternal Kingdom, deserves to be cast in full light in order to celebrate, glorify and exalt the mercy of God.

May we welcome his example of holiness today as the Western

Church did in the past and as the rites of the Eastern Church still do today!

The Good Thief, along with Thérèse of Lisieux, could become the "saint of the third millennium," an icon of the merciful love preparing the new Pentecost of love for which we are awaiting. "All of us are called to holiness." This beautiful statement from Vatican II runs a great risk of falling into oblivion again if the Church's teaching and pastoral work does not give sufficient consideration to the testimony of the "only saint" who Christ was keen on canonizing in fulfillment of his great plan of mercy. His merciful love freely accepted is what transforms and re-creates us. God's gift is freely given and is undeserved. The Good Thief brings us back to the cross, to Calvary, and tells us again that it is truly "through him, with him and in him" that we become saints.

Blessed Thief! Holy Good Thief! By responding to grace, he offers his Lord and Savior the opportunity of adding a page to his testament—where his infinite mercy bursts forth. Throughout all ages, it will have drawn to itself a procession of countless converted men and women, will have brightened so many agonies, comforted so many despairing or broken hearts, wrenched so many wretched people from the abyss, and raised so many saints.[86]

Yes, he is a model of holiness offered to all. We have entered into a period of great mercy. These graces, apparently reserved for great souls, will be poured into the lowliest ones. We will find, among the saints, weak and vulnerable children with wounded hearts. The Church, in her mystery, will perhaps experience an agony and a crucifixion, but a new Pentecost of love will burst forth through poverty and lowliness.

The great masters of prayer in the gospel are recognized by the Eastern Church as the Good Thief and the publican. This is because Jesus answered the Thief's prayer instantly by taking him into paradise, and because of Jesus' response to the publican's prayer, "God, be merciful to me, a sinner!"— "I tell you, this man went down to his home justified rather than the other, for all who exalt themselves will be humbled, but all who humble themselves will be exalted" (Luke 18:13-14).

God's holiness is the power of his love for the weak, the poor, the sick and the sinners. Is not the Good Thief's cry: "Jesus, remember me" the same as the publican's prayer: "God, be merciful to me, a sinner"? Holiness is openness to love. To love is not to be first heroic, but to let ourselves be seduced by love, to offer ourselves and to receive the gift of God. We do not build or fashion love, we receive it with a poor and humble heart.

The holy Good Thief teaches us that the gates of holiness are open to the poor and lowly. He makes these words from St. Paul real: "God chose what is foolish in the world to shame the wise; God chose what is weak in the world to shame the strong" (1 Corinthians 1:27).

The Good Thief is a saint whom we can and should invoke and on whom we ought to meditate. We hear through him the universal divine message, which is astonishingly applicable to our times. This message is, first, the extraordinary manifestation of mercy, then the hope of salvation and finally the call to holiness for all of us. This call summons those who have been hurt the most, the poorest and even those who lived away from God and the practice of their faith for years, as well as all those who are excluded, and sinners. "Praying...the Good Thief," said Cardinal Saliège, "is to make an act of humility; it is to set ourselves in our rightful place, the place of sinners."

The Holiness of Empty Hands

Those who have been hurt by life, those who are unloved, captives, those imprisoned in their passions, the distressed, the despairing—sinners—all find a brother in this Holy Thief.

The Good Thief's spirituality reminds us that we are capable of sinking into all the vices and of committing all the crimes. It teaches us to take our place as the vilest of sinners and it opens our whole being to the grace of God that produces holiness. The Good Thief tells us again that we must be open before God as the poorest of the poor, who have nothing to give him and who can only receive. The Good Thief shows us the purest example of Christian salvation that there is in the Gospel.

What an affront to our self-complacency and pride to think that the poorest and most rejected being, even a human derelict, can become a saint, provided he opens himself totally, like a void, to the action of redeeming grace!

The Good Thief, this model from the gospel, offers every man and woman a message of hope. He shows us that, through faith, hope and charity, we can take possession of the infinite merits of Jesus, of his life, death and resurrection. He shows us how to acknowledge that the sacred wounds of Jesus and his precious blood are the only gate to heaven that is always open to the poor who humbly admit they have nothing to offer or to pay for their admission.

Learning to Steal

The Good Thief, this "holy thief," can teach us to steal. What is stealing? It is to take possession of what does not belong to us. We do not have the right to rob material and earthly goods because we can procure them for ourselves through our labor and industry. But since it is absolutely impossible for man to procure heaven for himself through his own efforts or works, there is only one way of possessing it someday, and that is by "stealing" it.

How can we steal heaven? By simply acknowledging that there is no way for us to save and sanctify ourselves, to be divinized by our own means, nor "earn" or buy this treasure with the currency of our merits. "I will come before you with empty hands," said Thérèse of Lisieux.

Rudolph the Carthusian, in his *Vie de Jésus Christ*, after he had reproduced the praise given by the Church Fathers to the holy Good Thief, transcribed this beautiful prayer from Venerable Bede.

> *I beseech you, Lord, grant me first to recognize you as did the Good Thief, and by recognizing you, to acknowledge that I am a sinner and to glorify you who, although innocent, suffered for sinners. Grant me, I beg you, Lord, to desire, ask and obtain what the Good Thief was asking of you: "Remember me, Lord, when you are in your Kingdom." Amen*

Justice, according to the gospel, is mercy. This justice, as described in the parable of the laborers of the final hour, is strange. It fills those who, having labored all day with indignation when they see the laborers of the eleventh hour receiving the same salary as given to them. They protest and they are shocked. The holy Good Thief is the supreme manifestation of the justice of God, for his justice is mercy for sinners.

Salvation Is Offered to the Poor

In the end it is faith, as Paul says, which is the essential thing, for in the end it is Jesus Christ who saves. One is not saved by the inner experience. Salvation is not something we give ourselves. The problem is not to find the best instructor in the methods of the inner life. As St. Paul says: all have sinned and need the grace of God; the most "interiorized" sage as much as the most "exteriorized" ordinary sinner, because it is grace that saves, not interior life. It is the attitude of those who say: it doesn't matter what dogma you believe, the important thing is to be men of interior life. Now, we say just the opposite. The essential thing is that Jesus Christ has brought us salvation and, in reality, that is the only thing that saves. To be men of interior life, well, we must try to be so as much as possible; we do what we can. But it is the glory of the Christian affirmation that in it salvation is also offered to the poor. Salvation is not simply the privilege of a little elite, but of all who have come to believe in Jesus Christ. The mercy of Jesus Christ is this, that salvation is not reserved for mystics and is not the result of techniques of interiorization. And that is a wonderful thing!

Cardinal Daniélou
Myth and mystery

Chapter 6

The Good Thief and Mary: Refuge for Sinners

L uke the evangelist is the only gospel writer who relates the story of the Good Thief. How and from whom did he learn about it?

In the prologue of his gospel he states that he was keen on being informed of everything, from the beginning, from "eye-witnesses and servants of the Word" (Luke 1:1-2).

Among the possible eyewitnesses he refers to we must first think of Mary. According to custom, she had been authorized to come close to Jesus' cross as the mother of the condemned. Therefore she probably witnessed the change occurring in the heart of the Thief.

Pope John Paul II said:

> *Mary was called in a special way to bring close to people, that love which He had come to reveal: the love that finds its most concrete expression vis-à-vis the suffering, the poor, those deprived of their own freedom, the blind, the oppressed and sinners (On the Mercy of God, n° 9).*[87]

Mary, described as being "full of grace," is the compassionate woman, the mother of mercy.

Luke, the author of the texts revealing the Annunciation, the Visitation and the Presentation of Jesus at the Temple, refers explicitly to Mary's confidence and testimony, as she who "treasured all these things in her heart" (Luke 2:51).

Moreover, thanks to Luke's text, we can contemplate Mary as standing at the foot of the Jesus' cross, nearby the two criminals, fully exercising her maternal compassion and mediation.

It is through Mary's eyes that F. Faber contemplated the agony of the two criminals:

> *Sorrow widens great hearts ... Mary had adopted the thieves for sons. She needed children. She felt their value then in the same way we know the value of friend when we are losing him. His dying face shows us his worth, and means more than his living expression did. She struggled in prayer for those two scoundrels.*[88]

Mary, Daughter of Grace

Mary is a daughter of grace. What had she done to earn the privilege of giving the Word his humanity? She owes this to grace alone and not to some personal merit. Mary can therefore truthfully say, in the words of St. Paul: "By the grace of God I am what I am" (1 Corinthians 15:10).

The grace of God which has been showered on Mary is a "grace that comes to her from Christ," "the grace of God ... given ... in Christ Jesus" (1 Corinthians 1:4). Mary – and the Catholic Church declared this in the dogma of the Immaculate Conception – was preserved from sin "in view of the merits of Jesus Christ Saviour." In the *Magnificat*, Mary cries out: "My soul magnifies the Lord ... for the Mighty One has done great things for me." Mary attributes the wonders performed in her to God and his grace; she attributes no merits to herself.

Father Perrin, O.P., said:

Mary is a daughter of grace and she seems to proclaim this louder than Paul: "By the grace of God, I am what I am; his love has done everything for me." Mary's love is not like that of the sinning woman to whom much has been forgiven, it is unique, because everything was given to her. The privilege does not remove her from mercy; it shows that in her whole being, and from the first moment, the Virgin Mary was totally graced and gracious. The grace in Mary proclaims what she can do for us.[89]

In his book *Mary, Mirror of the Church,* Father Raniero Cantalamessa declares:

In the present-day technological culture we witness the elimination of the very idea of God's grace from human life. This is radical Pelagianism of modern mentality. Grace began to lose the extraordinary depth of meaning it had in the New Testament when, due to the error of the Pelagians, it was seen above all as a necessary help to man's weak will.[90]

Mary, Mary Magdalene and the Good Thief

When Mary was at the foot of the cross, she could see Mary Magdalene and grasp what Jesus' blood meant for her. Whereas Mary Magdalene could say, "O Precious Blood that cleanses me from my sin," the Virgin Mary could cry out, "O Precious Blood that has preserved me from all sin," as she watched the blood of her Son being shed.

Mary is the one who obtained mercy in a particular and exceptional way, as no other person has. At the same time, still in an exceptional way, she made possible through the sacrifice of her heart, her own participation in revealing God's mercy... No one has experienced, to the same degree as the Mother of the crucified One, the mystery of the cross, the overwhelming encounter of divine transcendent justice with love—that "kiss" given to justice by mercy. Mary, then, is the one who has the deepest knowledge of the mystery of God's mercy. She knows its price and she knows how great it is. It is in this sense that we call her the Mother of mercy.[91]

With Tears of Fire

Since the gospel tells us that one day "Jesus wept" (John 11:35), we may certainly think that the sorrowful Mother also wept. St. Catherine of Siena says also says that there are tears other than those of the eyes—the tears of the heart or of desire, which she calls tears of fire. At the foot of the cross Mary shed tears of fire, as she interceded for the salvation of sinners. "Tears of fire," Catherine of Siena points out, "are shed by the Holy Spirit in us."

Jesus was buoyed up by his love for sinners when, betrayed denied and abandoned by his friends, he was surrounded by those who were persecuting him, agonizing on the cross—and he forgave his enemies. Beyond any doubt Mary related the triumph of this mercy as revealed in the experience of the Good Thief to Luke. We might think that it would have been possible that Mary would die at the moment her Son died and that she would be the first to enter into paradise with Him—instead it was a criminal, a bandit who would be the "first of the elect." In his ineffable wisdom, God wanted Mary, as the Mother of mercy, to reveal what grace can accomplish in us even in the last moment of our life.

Mary, our Mother in the faith, is the Mother of the *Good Thief.* She would certainly want the "first one" to enter Heaven with her Son and to be recognized by the whole Church as having special significance for all who are desperate, marginalized, forsaken, and sinners crushed by the burden of guilt.

More than anyone else Mary entered into the perspective of mercy dominating the whole plan of creation. She herself was born "immaculate" out of sheer mercy, and she will never desire to be anything other than a pure herald of God's infinite mercy. So the Church gives her an almost proper name by calling her "Mother of mercy." Hence the special love she always displays towards the poorest, towards those who have been hurt by life, the lowly, and in a very special way the sinners afflicted by the worst of woes—sin. Like her Son, she has no concern other than the salvation of all people, hence the title "Refuge of sinners" that is still given to her by the Catholic Church.

Mary, the Compassionate Mother, and the Good Thief

On Calvary a relationship developed between the Good Thief and the compassionate Mary, as he turned to Jesus. She watched her Son, the fruit of her womb, offer himself for the salvation of the world.

"Standing" at the foot of the Savior's cross, ultimately "standing" at the foot of the Good Thief's cross, Mary had just received the two thieves (with John ... and all of us) as her own children. Mary can only pray for these criminals by offering her sorrowful heart and her Son Jesus, *the Innocent One*. And we could say that the "*Mother of mercy*" is standing there, offering and entreating, as though "on the threshold of hell" for the salvation of those "in greatest need of mercy."

Is it only by chance that the evangelist Luke is the one who relates the Good Thief episode? The woman who related the events of Jesus' infancy to Luke related the episode of this thief who turned to the Saviour with his poverty and whose heart was swept with mercy in an instant. Should we not associate Mary, the Refuge of sinners, with the Good Thief?

The New Pentecost of Love

Does not the Good Thief, the saint of new beginnings, prepare the way for those holy apostles of the cross of whom Grignion de Montfort speaks? Fr. Monier said about the Montfortian consecration:

> *If you hand over all your merits, it is certain that you will arrive in Heaven with empty hands and you will have nothing to defend yourself.*

Grignion de Montfort spoke of saints who would come, and by whom a great renewal of the Church would take place.

> *They will be "little and poor in the world's esteem, and abased before all; but rich in the graces of God, which Mary shall distribute to them abundantly. They shall "crush the head of the devil and cause Jesus Christ to triumph" (True Devotion to Mary, n° 54).*

Marthe Robin proclaimed a new Pentecost of love that would set the world ablaze. Fr. Georges Finet, who founded the Foyers de Charité, said one day:

> *Mary, who gave her Son to the world for the first time on the day of Pentecost, will make him burst forth in the world by a new Pentecost of love. At that moment, the Blessed Virgin will not be the source of very great graces. The word source is too limited. It will be an effusion of torrents of graces that will fall on the entire world. In these times that are coming, the Church will be totally restored, after she has passed through the cross. The cross will make the new Pentecost of love burst forth. The action of the Blessed Virgin, the new Pentecost of love must break out in the entire world. How will the Holy Spirit be given? We do not know, but notably by the apostles of the end times (15 Dec. 1975).*

We must keep on hoping in spite of appearances, and we must believe that the Holy Spirit is always with his Church and that the cross always proclaims the resurrection.

In his writings, St. John of the Cross speaks of the *dark night of the soul*. Pope John Paul II, on 29 September 1989, dared to say that Christians must now be "witnesses of the dark night of the soul experienced by our society." The pope therefore does not hesitate to set a parallel between the dark night of John of the Cross and the darkness that characterizes our time.

We could speak of a collective darkness weighing down on humanity (and perhaps on a part of the Church). We are living in a world from which God seems to be absent.[91]

On Calvary, at the moment of night and darkness, the Good Thief turns to Jesus our Saviour and receives the promise of paradise. By his life and death he proclaims the first beatitude: "Blessed are the poor for yours is the Kingdom of Heaven."

It is in the poverty of means, in weakness, when we are no longer able to do anything on our own, that the "power of God" is manifested. We, like children, must always keep up our hope in spite of the darkness.

It is through the lowliness of the Marian way and the little way of the Good Thief and Thérèse of Lisieux that the Holy Spirit will act with power.

God Will Seek the Poor

Montfort was anticipating a great renewal; he was expecting fiery priests, merciful priests who, through Mary, through the cross and the poverty of means, would take part in a great renewal of the Church. He said that these priests "would burn like fires and shed light like suns."

Will we not soon see these apostles of mercy modeled on the Good Thief? Like him, they will have been on the verge of despair, they will have been purified by trials, ridiculed by the world; but, converted in an instant by the grace of Jesus Christ. Having nothing to offer but their poverty, they will place their hope in Jesus Christ the son of Mary.

"Pride is what keeps us from being saints," said the holy Curé of Ars (St. Jean-Marie Vianney). Mary, at the foot of the cross, becomes the Mother of compassion, the Mother of the poor and sinners. She is preparing these saints of tomorrow. We will have surprises. God does not perceive things like we do: "God chooses what is low and despised in the world" (1 Corinthians 1:27).

Several years ago, Jean Daujat wrote the following words which I dare describe as prophetic:

> *If someday Christians simply became the most successful and the most admired of men, filled with natural talents and virtues, crowns of human achievement, then God would withdraw completely*

*from them and seek the poor, the lame, the
misshapen, the imbeciles, and all the human dere-
licts. Through the almighty power of the cross of
Jesus Christ, he would make saints of them and,
through them; he would transform the face of the
earth. When good Christians, like the Pharisees of
the gospel, become proud of their morality and their
virtues, and no longer see themselves as poor
sinners constantly in need of the mercy and power of
God, then, I declare to you, God will go and seek the
bandits and the prostitutes. By the almighty power of
the cross of Jesus Christ, he will make saints of them
and, through them; he will renew the face of the
earth. Then there will burst before the eyes of all the
fact that whoever glorified in himself is lost, and that
salvation and holiness lie only in the infinite worth
and the eternal triumph of the cross of Jesus Christ,
our only hope.*[92]

Every time the Church invites us to contemplate the crucified
Jesus with the eyes of the Blessed Virgin, it is to bring about our
conversion. Mary, the "almighty intercessor," as the Church
reminds us, shows us a model of holiness accessible to all. The
holiness of the Good Thief is the holiness of the *true* Church of the
poor, of the abased, the ridiculed, and the despairing. It is the holiness of these "thieves" that we all are at the moment of our death.

Mary helps us discover the holiness of the Good Thief like a
beacon of hope in the night of our world. God wants to choose the
lowly and the poor to consume them in the fire of his merciful love.

The great poet Claudel became amazed and overwhelmed as he
meditated on the Good Thief and exclaimed:

*"Today, you will be with me in Paradise" Today! In
one instant he is not only forgiven, but also sanctified! The assassin, the immodest and the thief, the
convict, the professional bandit has become a saint.
One gaze through these bleeding eyelids was enough*

*to trigger in the invited one on his right this cata-
clysm of repentance, this resurrection mixed with the
agony, this irresistible explosion of eternity. Today,
you will be with me in paradise. The deed is done.
Thus the prophecy that the publican would precede
us in the Kingdom of Heaven has been fulfilled to the
letter. In this vast space (of paradise), for the time
being, there is no one but he, he is all alone. He is
still the only one who has arrived. The Immaculate's
throne is still empty. He is there, in paradise, still
reeking alcohol and personal products, the first fruit.
Here is the one for whom the blood of a God has
been used.*[93]

The way of holiness for all of us will be the way of nothingness,
of emptiness, because this is the way of Mary, the pauper *par excellence.* This was the way of repentance represented by this criminal
crucified beside Jesus. Basically, a man is a saint inasmuch as he
perceives the distance that separates him from God. The holiest of
saints are often those who feel most acutely that they are sinners.
This is what the Good Thief teaches us. Sylvanus of Mount Athos
said: "I saw hell and paradise; they are already present here below!"

May Jesus through Mary, Refuge of sinners, help us discover
the little way of the Good Thief. May he help us live this absolute
poverty, this detachment from ourselves so that we may offer, like
the Good Thief, empty hands and a contrite heart in response to
infinite love.

Mary, Mother of the Forsaken ...

Mary, with Jesus, is turned entirely to those whom Jesus saves: all of humanity. All of humanity, that is all the sinners. Mary adopts them in her heart. Not a single sinner is a stranger to her.

Thus, because she has lived the mystery of the cross and has done so with a unique intensity, thanks to the mystery of the Immaculate Conception, Mary becomes the Mother of all the most unfortunate and the most forsaken. Mary is the one who, with Jesus, bears all the iniquity and all the misery of the world. Mary has this unique privilege of being only mercy. Mary received from God this grace that enables her never to have any aversion for the greatest sinners and to surround them. Mary is the one who has received from God this unique grace of being the 'Refuge of sinners'.

In her mercy for sinners, Mary cloaks them with the mercy of Christ, with the mercy of the Father. She unites to her heart, in a favored and special love, all those who are the most forsaken and the most rejected. This is her role as a Mother, as a Refuge of sinners. In her heart, Mary makes no distinction, as we do, between those who are chosen because they have been preserved and those who are chosen because they are the poorest, the most forsaken. In her heart, they have the same space and they are loved. Mary's divine motherhood brings together in one mystery her motherhood with regards to John and her motherhood with regards to the greatest sinners and those who are most forsaken: they are united in the same love.

Marie-Dominique Philippe, O.P.,
L'Étoile du matin, Fayard

Chapter 7

The Good Thief and Thérèse of Lisieux: A Similar Spirituality

We speak about the "childlike way" in connection with Thérèse, and we insist on the charm of childhood, but we could say just as well: the "way of the Good Thief."[95]

This statement from Céline, who is recognized as someone who speaks in ways that are in harmony with the mind and heart with Thérèse, deserves our in depth study. What enables us to accept Céline's words is the conclusion we draw from the words the Good Thief addresses to Jesus: "Remember me when you come into the brilliance of your Kingdom." What humility! What faith in Jesus' merciful love!

Thérèse is the doctor *par excellence* of merciful love, trust and surrender. From what we know of the end of his life the Good Thief, by his very being, reflects the same message—a message of salvation and life. The link Céline makes between the saint of Lisieux and the saint on Calvary appears to be the intuition of a genius and is worth exploring to the maximum. To do this properly, we need to note those passages in Thérèse's writings speaks explicitly of the Good Thief, and perhaps some other relevant passages as well. We will analyze these texts and make a coherent synthesis of all of them. Yes, that will be worth doing ...[96]

In *La Fuite en Égypte* (cf. RP 6) Thérèse exalts the mercy of the hidden God that even persecution sends as Redeemer before all men. This represents one of the rare passages in her works where she speaks explicitly of the Good Thief, or more precisely of the future Good Thief.

The way of childhood is offered as much to the Good Thief as to the Holy Innocents. Mary, the Mother of mercy, knows well the divided heart of men:

> *Nonetheless, place your trust in the infinite mercy of God: it is vast enough to obliterate the greatest crimes when it finds a motherly heart that places all its trust in it.*

Herein is a reflection of the little way, which is of such prime importance that Thérèse repeats it at the moment of her death, and which is the conclusion of her final manuscript:

> *I'm certain of this—that if my conscience were burdened with all the sins it's possible to commit, I would still go and throw myself into our Lord's arms, my heart all broken up with contrition: I know what tenderness he has for any prodigal son of his that comes back to him.*[97]

Céline notes that St. Thérèse followed the same "little way" as the Good Thief. Like him, she relied only on Jesus' merciful love to reach the summit of love; not on her own personal efforts, which are only there to increase her desire to love him and draw his evident help to herself. Like him, she does not rely on her own merits or works, since she thinks of arriving in Heaven with "empty hands."

When she entered Carmel, at the end of 1894, Céline brought a little notebook where she had written the texts from the Old Testament to which Thérèse had not yet had access and which would henceforth be determining factors in her elaboration of spiritual doctrine. Indeed, she found the well known text: "You that are simple, turn to me" (Proverbs 9:4), which resounded in her like a true "substantial word." Similarly the text: "I will extend prosperity to her like a river, and the wealth of the nations like an overflowing stream; and you shall nurse and be carried on her arm, and dandled on her knees" (Isaiah 66:12). From that time on, she began signing herself as "very little," giving the expression a strong spiritual significance.

In order that the way of spiritual childhood may be seen in a truly universal dimension, in order that no doubt may remain in those who are bound by moral misery, it is helpful to associate this contemporary apostle of merciful love with the holy Thief. In fact, Thérèse is seen as being so close to God that it would be possible for many people to overlook her teaching if it were not confirmed by the brigand in whom God revealed his mercy in such a powerful way.

Thérèse was fully aware of this when she said:

> *One could believe that I have such a great trust in God because I did not sin. Believe me Mother, even if I had all the crimes that can be committed on my conscience, I would lose none of my trust. With my heart broken with contrition, I would go and throw myself in the arms of my Savior. I know that he cherishes the prodigal son; I heard his words to St. Magdalene, to the adulteress, to the Samaritan woman. No, no one could frighten me, for I know what to think about my love and His Mercy. I know that this multitude of offences would fall into the abyss in the wink of an eye, like a drop of water in a burning blaze.*[98]

All her thought and spiritual deductions about the free gift of merciful love are exemplified in the Good Thief. And she boldly exclaims:

> *My protectors of Heaven and my favorite ones are those who stole it, like the Holy Innocents and the Good Thief. The great saints earned it with their works; as for myself, I want to imitate the thieves, I want to have it through the guile and wiles of love that will open the entrance to me, to me and to poor*

sinners. The Holy Spirit encourages me, since he says in the Proverbs: "O simple ones learn prudence from me!" (8:5).[99]

In spite of the fact that the texts of Thérèse concerning the Good Thief are rare, those writings are nevertheless sprinkled with a multitude of meaningful words about God's great plan of merciful love. If Thérèse had considered those lowly souls who follow the way of spiritual childhood, she would not cast aside great sinners themselves from this bold hope. She wrote to Fr. Bellière on 21 June 1897:

How could our sins not be consumed beyond return when we throw them with a totally filial trust into the consuming fire of Love?

You love St. Augustine, St. Magdalene, these souls to whom many sins were forgiven because they loved a great deal ... And I love them, I love their repentance and especially ... their loving boldness!

When I see Magdalene move forward, I feel that her heart has understood the abysses of love and mercy in the Heart of Jesus. Sinner as she is, she knows that this Heart of love is not only disposed to forgive her, but also to lavish upon her the blessings of his divine intimacy and raise her to the highest summits of contemplation.

Ah! How I would like to make you understand the tenderness of the Heart of Jesus! (18 July 1897).

Father, how little the kindness and the merciful love of Jesus are known! It is true that, to enjoy these treasures, we must abase ourselves and acknowledge our nothingness. And that is what many souls do not want to do (26 July 1897).

As for the Good Thief, he abased himself, acknowledging that he was a great sinner. He looked at Jesus and found his gaze full of tenderness and mercy. Again, as Thérèse says:

> *When Jesus has casts his eye on a soul, he immedi-*
> *ately grants it his divine resemblance, but this soul*
> *must not cease to fix its eyes on him alone (to Céline,*
> *26 April 1892).*

Forced to discontinue writing in July 1897 because of weakness, she asked Mother Agnès to complete her manuscript with the story of the sinning woman who died of love. "The souls will understand straightaway, it is such a striking example of what I would like to say."[100]

Like Thérèse, the Good Thief understood "that one only had to seize Jesus through his heart," and he was given the privilege to "become the prey of his Love," to be "plunged for eternity into the burning abyss of Love to which he offered himself as a victim."[101]

We detect the filigree-like silhouette of the Good Thief in Thérèse's letters:

> *Céline, it seems to me that God does not need*
> *years to accomplish his work of love in a soul. A*
> *beam from his heart, can in an instant cause his*
> *flower to bloom for eternity.*[102]
>
> *It seems to me that love can supplement a long*
> *life ... Jesus does not consider time, since time no*
> *longer exists in Heaven, he must consider only*
> *love.*[103]
>
> *I feel that I will never be [ready] unless the Lord*
> *himself deigns to transform me. He can do so in an*
> *instant. After all the graces he has showered on me,*
> *I am still awaiting that of his infinite Mercy.*[104]

An acknowledged misery is like a lever, an elevator rising up to the Heart of God, compelling him to deploy the torrents of His mercy.

Thérèse wants to reveal that what is most miserable, weakest, and least lovable—whether on the physical, psychological or spiritual level—is perhaps our greatest treasure in drawing near to the open Heart of God.

If we consider the resemblance between Thérèse and the Good Thief from the perspective and acknowledgement of our own misery and our total trust in God's love, we think again of these essential texts in Thérèse's writings:[105]

> *I think that if, against all possibility, you found a soul weaker than mine, you would be pleased to shower it with still greater favors, if it surrendered itself in total trust to your infinite Mercy (Ms B, 5 v°).*

> *What pleases [God] is to see me love my lowliness and my poverty, it is the blind hope that I have in his Mercy [...]. It is trust, and only trust that must lead us to Love ... Fear does not lead to justice, to the austere justice, as it is represented to sinners, but to this Justice that Jesus will have for those who love him.*[106]

> *We obtain from him as much as we hope for.*[107]

> *I hope as much from God's Justice as from his Mercy. Because he is just, he is compassionate and filled with gentleness, slow to chastise and abundantly merciful, for he knows our fragility. He remembers that we are but dust. Like a father who is tender towards his children, so the Lord has compassion for us.*[108]

While the name of the Good Thief does not appear textually in Thérèse's teaching, we must remember that by the nineteenth century, he had disappeared almost completely from recognition within the Western Christian World. Yet Thérèse had been enthusiastic about Pranzini. She had prayed for him and asked for a sign of his conversion and had obtained it! In the *Manuscrit autobiographique*, we read over the account of his death:

He turned, seized a crucifix presented to him by the priest and kissed his sacred wounds three times. Then his soul went to receive the merciful sentence ...[109]

How could Thérèse not have thought of the Good Thief as she wrote these lines?

In her *Act of Offering to the Merciful Love*, Thérèse exclaimed:

Lord, I am not asking you to number my works. All our justices are tainted in your sight. I therefore want to cloak myself with your own justice and receive from your love the eternal possession of your own being [...]. Time is nothing in your sight; a single day is like a thousand years. You can therefore in one instant prepare me to appear before you. I feel my helplessness and I ask you, O my God, to be yourself my holiness.[110]

There you have childhood at its summit: *that of the Good Thief!* Thérèse's *Act of Offering* could just as well be signed by the Good Thief. After having experienced it on his gibbet, did he not proclaim it at the moment of his death?

Thérèse's whole work ought to be studied. But the most moving echo, perhaps, the purest and truest, is found in Thérèse's response addressed to her godmother:

Where can we find the truly poor in spirit? We must look for him very far away, said the psalmist. He does not say we must search for him among the great souls, but "very far away," that is, in lowliness, in nothingness. Trust, and only trust, must lead us to Love... Yes, I feel it, Jesus wants to give us his Heaven freely.[111]

Love Wants to Be Spread ...

The way of the Good Thief is the "little way," the immediacy of mercy. The weakness we have to offer must be opened to the fire of merciful love. In the Good Thief, Thérèse of Lisieux discovers that God yearns for hearts that are poor in spirit, who desire to receive his love just as He wishes to give it. To love God is to open one's heart to receive his love in order to be consumed by it.

God, the mendicant of love, stands like a pauper at the door of our hearts. Olivier Clément says these beautiful words: "Open the door of your heart to the mendicant of love knocking on it."

Would not the most beautiful gift we can possibly offer to God be to receive his love and drink at his source? "God is the spring that thirsts to be drunk," said St. Gregory of Nyssa.

It is interesting to read the testimony given by Thérèse's sister, Sister Agnès, during the apostolic proceedings, about the offering to merciful love.

> *Seeing to what extent the love of God is misunderstood on earth, she was inspired to offer herself to this merciful love. She meant by that to offer her heart to God as an abyss that she would have wanted to be infinite to contain the flames of divine charity that are rejected by most, and to be consumed by them to the point of dying from love.*

> *In turn, Sister Geneviève declared during the same proceedings:*

> *By this act she was asking God to pour into her the love he wanted to pour into this world and that creatures refused to receive.*

An Act for the Elite or for the Poor?

We must associate the Good Thief with Thérèse in order to be able to present this *Act of Offering* and to make it accessible to the hurt, the poor, the lowly, and even to sinners.

Thérèse's little way is also the Good Thief's little way. Therefore, her *Act of Offering* is not reserved for the elite, much to the contrary. That is why Thérèse does not wait until souls no longer have any shortcomings in order to offer them to the merciful, consuming and transforming love. On the contrary, she surrenders them to this love because they are filled with woes and feel unable to amend themselves on their own. The only condition set by Thérèse for this offering to be effective is the very one—the only one—that God lays down for the fruitfulness of the Redemption. It is "the poverty of heart, true humility, the acknowledgement of one's condition as a sinner, a total surrender in trust to the merciful love."

That is exactly what the holy Good Thief did. And yet, when some spiritual directors present this *Act of Offering* as something very special, reserved for the "spiritual elite," they are, without being too aware, at totally opposite poles from the Theresian spirit.

Thérèse said: "Everything I have done [therefore including the *Act of Offering*], I want all the lowly souls to be able to do." Was not this "tiny little soul," "weak and imperfect" first and foremost that of the "Good Thief," the "thief of paradise," as Thérèse noted?

She who would have wanted to live in a refuge with former prostitutes would certainly not have wanted her spirituality to be presented as being for the elite or for great generous souls. She said:

> *If I had not been accepted at Carmel, I would have entered a refuge to live there unknown and scorned in the midst of former prostitutes and poor "repentant" people.*

> *My happiness would have been to be considered as such by all who would have seen me; I would have been the apostle of my companions, telling them what I think of God's mercy.*

Thérèse offers us an example that, like the Good Thief, is truly the opposite of Pharisaism. Instead of saying: "I thank you that I am not like the other people," she wanted to be seen by all as a former prostitute. Unfortunately, and contrary to Thérèse of Lisieux and the Good Thief, many Christians think they are rich by their own merits and virtues, just like the Pharisee of the gospel. They think they are able to grow in their spiritual life simply by their own personal efforts or natural virtues.

The book of Revelation provides the answer:" You say: 'I am rich, I have prospered, and I need nothing.' You do not realize that you are wretched, pitiable, poor, blind and naked" (Rev 3:17).

Father Louis Sankalé comments:

> *Let us also think of the Good Thief, this man who failed at everything, except in the last second, and who enters paradise ahead of everyone (Luke 23:43). This is true for him, it is true for Thérèse, and for us as well!*[112]

In a flash of intuition, the Good Thief understood that holiness is not the fruit of personal effort, but of grace granted by God. In the crucified Jesus he recognized the personification of love that abases itself to the point of offering his life to redeem us and to give us the gift of the Spirit, thus making us capable of loving as he does—in truth. By discovering Jesus and entrusting the burden of the past to His mercy, the Good Thief staked everything on him: he chose him at the ultimate limit of his life and openly confessed his kingdom. He magnified his Lord.

On the spot, in serene peace, Jesus honors him with his trust—he who thought himself unworthy of that is the first to enter paradise immediately with Jesus! In him, there is no trace of Pharisaism or self-complacency ... He had become one of those "very lowly" souls to whom the Father gives his Kingdom freely.

Indeed, how can we doubt the holiness *in extremis* in this sinner, in the tragic circumstances that surrounded the sorrowful and supreme sacrifice of the Redemption? But also what a consolation for Jesus in his appalling suffering, when he saw that his coming death was already bearing fruit—and what fruit! At this moment, the Virgin Mary must have sensed and understood the wonders that God was preparing for those who humble themselves and let themselves be filled by love, be it at the final moment!

The acknowledgement that Thérèse of Lisieux can make the way of trust in divine mercy better known and once again helps elevate the Good Thief to the rightful higher place that should his in Christian devotion.

The spirituality exemplified in the lives of Thérèse and the Good Thief rests on four essential elements: *humility*, *lowliness* (the sense of that is connatural to the poor), *trust* and *surrender*.

If we consider the Good Thief, we understand that God is only love and mercy.

The connection between Thérèse and the Good Thief thus appears to be, as it were, God's great plan for our time—a great plan of mercy. Thérèse's teaching is reinforced by the Good Thief's behaviour in which God has revealed his infinite mercy in such a dazzling way. He is really the most significant figure of the "gratuity" and universality of offered by Christ, the Redeemer to all people for their salvation.

Conclusion

The charter of the "little way" is addressed to all sinners, as well as to the poor and the suffering of our world.

If Thérèse of Lisieux enables us discover the fatherhood of God and his mercy, the Good Thief is the most significant figure of the gratuity and universality of the salvation that Christ, the Redeemer, offers to us.

Holy Good Thief, pray for us, poor sinners.

Whoever Acknowledges His Misery …

"For Jesus to be merciful there must be someone who is miserable, a beggar, a poor individual, someone who acknowledges his misery, his weakness and who deposits it in his heart.

"Nowadays, the devil is trying to make man believe that he can save himself and that he no longer needs Christ. When Christ came the first time, there was no room for him at Bethlehem. Now, it is more serious, for there is no longer any room for Christ as Savior.

"What is the great temptation today: to believe that we can discover methods that enable us to save ourselves. This is terrible, because man no longer admits he is a sinner, and so he can no longer receive the mercy of the Holy Spirit and Christ. We are often faced with this temptation and we do not see it. We let ourselves be had by it, by agreeing that someone other than Christ can save us."

Fr. Marie-Dominique Philippe
L'Acte d'offrande

Chapter 8

The Good Thief and Christian Liturgy

The Second Vatican Council recommended that "only those [feasts] should be extended to the universal Church which commemorates saints who are truly of universal importance" (*SC* n° 111). There are probably no saints to whom this recommendation is more appropriate than the Good Thief. Is it not surprising that, in the Catholic Church, only an ordinary Mass of devotion has been conceded to this saint of the gospel?

It seems fitting for us to affirm that the ultimate witness of divine mercy is this saint for all people for all times and perhaps especially for our time.

His example can only be beneficial for each one of us. His presence at the sacrifice on Calvary should help us gain a better grasp of the unfathomable mystery of Christ's Passover, in order to better live out our own participation in the Eucharist.

His faith, his patience in suffering, the acceptance of his cross out of love for God are some other personal spiritual fruits that the Good Thief demonstrates. When the burden of our misery generates despair, his example will inspire us toward a total trust in the infinite divine mercy.

But beyond these motives of the natural order—which are easily listed—there are others of a universal order which speak in favor of widely extending devotion to the Good Thief.

First, we have in mind the divine aspects of the actual and universal mission of the Church; then the importance of venerating the Good Thief on the ecumenical level; and finally the eschatological dimension of the gospel message, which is little understood.

Devotion to the Good Thief

This devotion is rooted in the tradition of the Fathers of the Church. This has a long history that we shall briefly review.

First, the writings of the Fathers of the Church are surprising. Their eloquence is inexhaustible and their admiration for this Thief who has won their sympathy is unanimous.

"Insatiable for details, inexhaustible in praise, they have lavished a special tenderness on him," writes Fr. Bessières. Why such effusions and such a vital interest?

The tradition they have handed down to us is striking in that it sets forth the sound basis of devotion to the one St. John Chrysostom calls "the figure and the precursor of all the elect."[112] In fidelity to their teaching, the Church has surrounded him for centuries with great veneration.

Without being named, the Good Thief was first mentioned in the Eastern Church's Synaxarion of Constantinople sometime during the ninth or tenth century.

The commentary, that is read at the beginning of the Mass in honor of the holy Thief is found in the Proper of Jerusalem and indicates that as early as the tenth century his devotion was established at Jerusalem.

In the Christian Churches of Syria and Iraq (formerly Mesopotamia), his feast is celebrated on the Saturday of Easter week. The Greeks, on their part, commemorate him on 23 March and, finally, among Latins, the martyrology has maintained remembrance of the Good Thief on 25 March, a date considered since the earliest Ancient times as the anniversary of Christ's death.[113]

In the Middle-Ages the Good Thief's popularity was very significant.

According to St. Peter Canisius, who traveled throughout

Belgium, Germany, Switzerland, Austria and Italy his liturgical cult spread progressively as many dioceses solemnized his feast day. He points out that his feast was also celebrated in the old cathedral of Bruges as in most churches.

During the sixteenth century, the Order of Our Lady of Mercy for the redemption of captives obtained approval for their liturgy of the Good Thief from Pope Sixtus the Fifth.

In the eighteenth century the Congregation of the Pious Laborers (Italy) obtained the same favor when they chose the Good Thief as the patron saint of their missions.

The Oblates of Mary Immaculate, the Servants of Mary, the Regular Clerics of St. Gaetano da Tiene also recited the liturgy of the Good Thief.

The Good Thief was also very popular in some regions of Spain and England and particularly in southern Italy.

Since the Second Vatican Council, the Good Thief has progressively been coming back to light in a special way. Thus, since 16 June 1971, he is celebrated on 12 October in the calendar of the Patriarchate of Jerusalem, a tradition already evident in the tenth century in the Palestinian Georgian calendar. His memory was subsequently added into the calendar of Lyon from 27 September 1976, then into the calendar of St. Flour from 20 November 1981. Since 27 July 1982, his Mass has been inserted in the collection of the votive masses of the Holy Land. It is celebrated in Jordan and Cyprus. In 1985, the Sacred Congregation for Divine Worship granted a Mass of the Good Thief to the National Chaplaincy of prisons in France.

A popular and moving devotion to the Good Thief may be found in many parts of the world, but especially in the Eastern Church and in Latin America.

Nowadays, priests respond in the name of Christ the Redeemer and the example of his response to the request of his companion in crucifixion by remembering him on their own while celebrating the Mass—a memorial of the Passion of Christ. Is not remembering the Good Thief a way of proclaiming divine mercy and invoking divine mercy for all of us? And is this not testifying again to the hope that is in us?

What the Popes Think ...

We have quoted excerpts from the sermons of Pope St. Leo the Great, who testified to his amazement at the gift of faith granted to the Good Thief. So did St. Gregory the Great, Pope and doctor of the Church, not to speak of contemporary Popes.

Pius XII saw in Jesus' almighty mercy, granted to his companion in crucifixion, the grace of an immediate conversion and the promise of a beatification implied in his answer—"almost the first plenary indulgence granted by Christ himself" (5 December 1954).

As a result of the fascinating historical evolution during the last four or five centuries, the Church of Jesus, under the action of his Spirit, has extended this promise to everyone. This is granted to all the well-disposed baptized in the form of a plenary indulgence at the hour of their death, even in the absence of a priest.

> *If a priest is not available, the Church grants a plenary indulgence to the faithful in danger of dying, on condition that he is properly disposed and has been in the habit of reciting some prayers during his life.*[114]

Paul VI was also keen on invoking the Good Thief by name in his proclamation of the *Credo*:

> *From the moment when the souls of those who die in the grace of Christ leave their body, Jesus takes them to Paradise as he did for the Good Thief ... (30 June 1968).*

The Good Thief, the Cross and the Mass

Since we are dealing with liturgy, I wish to note that the Good Thief was present at the death of Jesus on the cross and was transformed. But are we aware that we are also present there, as really as he was, every time we attend the Eucharistic sacrifice? On 30 June 1968, in his profession of faith (the aim of which was to respond to the errors of certain theologians concerning the Mass) Pope Paul VI clearly stated:

> *We believe that the Mass which is celebrated by the priest representing the person of Christ, in virtue of the power he receives in the Sacrament of Order and which is offered by him in the name of Christ and of the members of his Mystical Body, is indeed the Sacrifice of Calvary sacramentally realized on our altars.*

The essential part of the Mass is the consecration, for the consecration of the Eucharist, through means of the sacrament and in faith makes us attend and participate in the redeeming sacrifice. A sacrament is a sign that performs what it means—the consecration of the Eucharist *actualizes the sacrifice of the cross.* We are therefore as present there as were Mary, St. John and the Good Thief.

The sacrifice of the Mass is not a sacrifice other than that of the cross; it is the sacrifice of the cross in the sacramental form represented by the sacrament. Do we still teach this? Do Christians know that there is a vast difference between a simple liturgy of the Word and the Mass, and that nothing can take the place of the *Eucharistic sacrifice*? This is not an old obsolete doctrine; it is a doctrine present in the four Eucharistic prayers.

The Mass therefore has *the same infinite value as the cross* as a source of graces and holiness since it is nothing other than the cross itself realized again in the form of the sacrament. The result is that the Mass should be the foundation of all our Christian life and that it is infinitely superior to all other religious practices, to all other works or deeds of whatever kind. We would be placing our works above the cross of Jesus Christ if we did not consider it as such.

The holy Curé of Ars said:

> *All the good works gathered together do not measure up to the holy sacrifice of the Mass, because they are the works of men and the Mass is the work of God. Martyrdom is nothing in compari-*

son to it, it is the sacrifice that Man makes of his life to God; the Mass is the sacrifice that God makes of his Body and Blood for man.

The Eucharist, a Sacrifice

Often when missionaries arrived in a new country, they would begin by planting a cross and celebrating *the sacrifice of the Mass*, the center of their own sacrifices for the formation of a Church. Everything holds together in the mystery of the cross: Christ and Christians; the historical Golgotha and the celebration of the Eucharistic sacrifice; and the offering of the sacred species and that of crucified lives. Everything revolves around the cross.

For several decades we have insisted on the dimension of a shared meal during the Eucharist, but we have perhaps forgotten that it is *a meal marked by a sacrifice*, mysteriously represented before us. For taking part in it also means sharing one's mystery of painful immolation in view of salvation. As John Paul II declared:

> *The Eucharist is above all else a sacrifice. It is the sacrifice of the Redemption and also the sacrifice of the New Covenant (On the Mystery and Worship of the Eucharist, 9. 24 February 1980).*

On his part Paul VI said:

> *By means of the Mystery of the Eucharist, the Sacrifice of the Cross, which was once offered on Calvary, is remarkably re-enacted and constantly recalled, and its saving power exerted for the forgiveness of those sins which we daily commit (Mysterium Fidei).*

The Second Vatican Council declared:

> *Our Savior, at the Last Supper, on the night when he was betrayed, instituted the Eucharistic sacrifice of*

> his Body and Blood to perpetuate the sacrifice of the
> cross throughout the ages until he comes (*Lumen
> Gentium, 7*).

Representing humanity on Calvary, a humanity that is gravely wounded by sin, the cross of the Good Thief must therefore be associated with that of Jesus. It is an urgent invitation to a total surrender to divine mercy. The example of the Good Thief, who was the first to take part in it in a direct way, makes this fact one of universal importance.

The memory of the Good Thief can be beneficial to each one of us. His presence at the sacrifice of Calvary enables us to have a better grasp of the unfathomable mystery of Christ's Passover and to participate in the Eucharistic sacrifice in a better way.

There is *only one* sacrifice worthy of God and salvific for the world—the sacrifice of the cross. That is why there is nothing greater than the Mass. This topic was developed precisely by Jacques Maritain:

> *The Almighty Divine Power, by means of the sacrifi-*
> *cial sign, makes real the sacrifice of the cross that is*
> *preserved eternally in heaven ... At the most solemn*
> *moment of the Mass, we are really present at the*
> *sacrifice of the cross as it took place in the past. But*
> *if this is so, it is because, through the (miraculous)*
> *effect of a ritual sign (with an existential dimension)*
> *that is accomplished on the altar, we are concretely*
> *and physically made present at this same sacrifice of*
> *the cross as it is preserved eternally in heaven ... By*
> *virtue of the sacrificial sign, a certain moment of our*
> *time participates miraculously in divine eternity and*
> *merges with a certain moment of a certain time of*
> *the past preserved in it (Approches sans entraves).*

When we help people understand that the Mass *makes the sacrifice of the cross actual*, we then invite sinners, thieves, prostitutes and all the criminals to come and offer themselves to the *divine*

Victim and receive countless graces, even conversion like that of the Good Thief—and that, without *necessarily receiving communion.*

Were You There?

"Were you there, were you there when they crucified my Lord?" says a most beautiful Negro spiritual. And it goes on: *"Sometimes it causes me to tremble, tremble, tremble!"*

The Good Thief causes us to cast a new look on the one we have pierced with our sins; to look with faith, repentance, and trust at Jesus on the cross. "Hail, O Cross, my only hope!" says a hymn of the Passion season.

From the Cross to the New Pentecost

The liturgy of the Good Thief enables us to rediscover the mystery and the supernatural efficacy of the cross. We must understand that the Good Thief is not a saint of diminished worth or the object of last minute luck. He was totally transformed by grace and he is a saint, a true saint, just as great a saint as Thérèse of Lisieux or St. Vincent de Paul. For, as Jean Daujat wrote:

> We must affirm, contrary to Luther, that this infinite holiness of the cross of Jesus Christ, without which we are irremediably sinners, does not leave us in the state of being sinners by giving us only a legal right to the attribution of salvation. It is truly communicated to us so that we may cease to be sinners and become truly and really saints through Jesus Christ and in him.[115]

In 1933, the Lord revealed to Martha Robin that the Church would recover her youth, that there would be a new spring and a new Pentecost of love, but that she would be asked to offer her life. For fifty years, Martha experienced the Passion in a self-effaced and discreet way. "After the material defeat of the nations," she said, "will come this new Pentecost of love."

However, before the resurrection of Christ and Pentecost, let us not forget that there was the Passion, the cross and the silence of the tomb!

If the Church is nothing but "Jesus spread and communicated," as Bossuet taught, she must, in turn, unite herself to the redeeming Passion of the Son of God crucified, before such a new Pentecost of Love can come.

When the Good Thief acknowledges his sins on Calvary and is assured of salvation, *darkness* covers Jerusalem. Barabbas is freed. The chief priests, the doctors and theologians are triumphant. *Humanly speaking*, this is a failure. The apostles have fled; only Mary, the Mother of Jesus, retains the faith of the Church in her sorrowful and immaculate heart. This is the hour of the *Good Thief* preceding the darkness of Holy Saturday and the resurrection of Easter morning, proclaiming the descent of the Holy Spirit on the Church. I believe that through the powerful example of the Good Thief we will soon have astonishing conversions, for "God will choose what is foolish to shame the wise" (1 Corinthians 1:27).

The Good Thief and Christian Unity

Are we Christians in the Western world, ready to give the Good Thief the place given to him by the Christians of the Byzantine tradition—especially the Russian Church– where Christian people see themselves in this moving figure of the "poor type who has faith" (Dostoyevsky)?

The Good Thief, indeed, may become a Covenant between the sister Churches of the West and the East, for he enjoys a huge popularity in the latter.

We are amazed at the central place that various Eastern rites— Byzantine, Alexandrine or Coptic, Syriac, Armenian, Maronite and Chaldean—have kept for him, close to the redeeming Christ. In the Byzantine liturgy the memory of the Good Thief is present everywhere.

Conclusion

A Hope for the Future

We are not in a position to discern clearly what the needs of the Church will be in coming years. We can however adopt the Good Thief as a model of holiness for our times.

Some Reflections

- Our world, fascinated by progress in science and technology is dominated by concerns for effectiveness, for profit-earning capacity, permissiveness, and for easy and immediate pleasure. Idols (money, drugs, sex, etc.) are proliferating. Our world is riveted to the earth, to present life, that overshadows death and especially life beyond. Through his torture, his prayer, his hope and through the response and promise of Jesus who heard his prayer, the Good Thief makes our eyes rise to the future and arouses our awareness of the proximity of the Kingdom of God.

- The Good Thief can become the saint of the third millennium because he is associated with Thérèse of Lisieux in teaching and spreading the "little way," the way of the gospel, the way of holiness for all, including the poorest, to whom God wants us to commit ourselves.

- The proclamation of Thérèse of Lisieux as doctor of the Church seems significant. Is this not an invitation that God is addressing to humanity to commit itself to the way of the spiritual childhood as it was lived by Thérèse and the Good Thief? And if, as Céline Martin (Sister Geneviève) recalled, Thérèse's spirituality is none other than that of the Good Thief, we have reason to think that they are associated together for a common mission in the Church that will prolong itself and expand in the years to come.

Thérèse's little way may become the way of holiness for the poor and even for repentant sinners. The Good Thief is associated with Thérèse because he expresses, by his very being and by what we know of the end of his life, the whole spirituality of the "little way."

- Definition of holiness according to the heart of God: it is *love*. (Do not confuse perfection and holiness.)

- Therefore, we are all called to holiness since we are made by love and for love, God being Love. Holiness is our vocation, our first duty of state (declaration of the Council).

- Christ is the first player in this. His love, accepted, is what transforms and re-creates us. Merits then emerge and grow relative to the time granted to us. Yet these "merits" are there only as an evidence or proof of our love for God.

- Holiness is timeless. "God does not need time to fulfill his work in a soul."

- The association of Thérèse and the Good Thief brings a truly universal dimension to the way of spiritual childhood.

- Their association is willed by God in view of the Pentecost of merciful love in order to prepare the civilization of love which John Paul II is calling for in his wishes and prayers.

- The Good Thief is the antidote to *Pelagianism*, which makes holiness and salvation depend on our personal merits, and to the Pharisaism of those who believe they are "righteous."

- The occult powers of this world today flaunt an exaggerated pride with impudence. They proclaim the death of God. Through deceitful propaganda, they condition the minds: good becomes evil, and evil becomes good. Virtue is ridiculed. Each makes himself the judge of his own conscience. Man deifies himself. We see the results of that.

Undoubtedly, God will oppose this Luciferian pride by raising legions of "little souls," as Thérèse of Lisieux says. We will see what St. Paul wrote in his first letter to the Corinthians become true:

> *God chose what is foolish in the world to shame the wise; God chose what is weak in the world to shame the strong; God chose what is low and despised in the world, things that are not, to reduce to nothing things that are, so that no one might boast in the presence of God. He is the source of your life in Christ Jesus, who became for us wisdom from God, and righteousness and sanctification and redemption, in order that, as it is written, "Let the one who boasts, boast in the Lord" (1 Corinthians 1:27-31).*

"My favorite saints: the Holy Innocents and the Good Thief." What intuition in Thérèse! The Holy Innocents who represent these millions of children who are born and exterminated. The Good Thief represents those who suffer over whom the threat of another plague hovers carrying the name of euthanasia. A timely devotion, therefore, to struggle effectively against the two plagues of our society: abortion and euthanasia.

- Are not the spirituality of the Good Thief, his death and Jesus' promise to bring him to paradise "on this very day," a response to the appealing idea of reincarnation, even among Christians? Christ does not say: "When you have experienced your karma, you will come to paradise"; Christ does not say: "After several reincarnations in different bodies, you will be with me in paradise"; Christ says: "On this very day."

For those who believe in reincarnation, the body does not have very much value; as for the soul, it is a principle which in each new existence changes its mode of being, and whose final destiny culminates ultimately in the great all. Thus "the unity of the human person as a unique and irreplaceable subject before God is challenged" (Bernard Sesboüé. S.J.). According to this idea, man is the one who makes the effort to acquire salvation and raise himself to the nirvana. He is the one who raises himself to God, and not God who saves man. Man is the one who saves himself through his efforts and merits. This is contrary to the gospel.

The words Jesus addresses to the Good Thief affirm the "unity" and irreplaceable worth of the person who plays out his or her eternal destiny in his or her *unique* earthly experience and who is called to salvation in the totality of their being: body and soul.

The Good Thief's attitude also shows that Jesus is the one who saves, that "God is the one who seeks man, who goes out to meet him, who wants to bring about through his mercy and love, a communion with man" (Bernard Sesboüé, S.J.).

The Good Thief answers the existential questions we all ask

ourselves and that modern man asks himself: Where do we come from? Who are we? Where are we going?

There is a powerful instinct in us that drives us to resist death. The Good Thief experienced it, as we all do. We can imagine what Jesus' promise must have meant for him: "Today, you will be with me in paradise."

We ought to study the Good Thief's death and Jesus' promise. We may then say that rediscovering the devotion to the Good Thief can help the Church and Christians to stay the course in the rising appeal of reincarnation and of other similar "spiritualities" brought in by the New Age movement. Is it not paradoxical to see in our times the massive loss of faith in all life after death, the rejection of all resurrection and at the same time to see the development, even among Christians, of ambiguous notions like reincarnation and certain similar currents of thought!

The Good Thief can become an example of Christian hope by helping us perceive the death and the cross of Christ in faith, as every true Christian must do.

> • The Good thief may also be considered as the leader of all the *marginalized*, of those who are cut off and even rejected from our societies, who are abandoned and scorned. John Paul II often recalls that the Church must keep this at the forefront in its commitment on their behalf.

Among the marginalized, there are first of all *AIDS victims* who are abandoned, sometimes even by their families, rejected and reviled, sometimes dying all alone, like pariahs. Who better than the Good Thief could be a model for them, especially at the time of their agony and death?

Prisoners belong to the world of the excluded. The Good Thief, who was one of them, is certainly in a good position to understand them, to love them and inspire pastoral initiatives to serve them. The Good Thief is the "protector" of prisoners and of those sentenced to death, for he knew and experienced their condition to the extreme limit. Like them, he was arrested, imprisoned, subjected to violent treatment, privations, to physical and moral torture; he was dragged, shackled, brought before a tribunal to be judged, no doubt in an expeditious way; he heard the terrible sentence of crucifixion fall on him. While he painfully worked his way through a hostile crowd, he had to put up with sarcastic remarks and with all kinds of projectiles thrown at him. He experienced the anguish of the wait, the piercing torment of the preparations, and the appalling pain of a death that dragged on for hours. And no doubt, he questioned himself about his eternal future, he, the outlaw, destined to hell by the collective good conscience.

Since he shared their condition, we can see in him the friend of those sentenced to death, their confidant, their advocate and their powerful intercessor with God.

Finally, when we listen carefully to what he says, first to his colleague, then to Jesus, we quickly understand that his initiative, directed both to the guilty and to the innocent, makes him the patron saint of all detainees, without exception.

When he addresses his colleague in robbery, does he not exhort him to acknowledge honestly his wrongs, and then hand himself over to God? This is an invitation to reconciliation.

He fearlessly defends Jesus in the face of his cynical accusers and proclaims his innocence.

Also, the memory of the Good Thief can only arouse initiatives in favor of the marginalized.

On the subject of prisoners, Christians should never forget to put these words from Jesus into practice: "I was in prison and you visited me!" (Mt 25:36).

Since 1981, a movement of great scope has been growing in France and is already spreading beyond its boundaries. It is the *Fraternité des prisons Bon Larron* (Prison Fellowship – Bon Larron) that has become an association of faithful. This movement gathers together Christians who are concerned about being effective brotherly companions for the detainees and their families during their detention and helping the ex-detainees on every level to facilitate their reintegration into society.

The originality and the dynamism of this fraternity rests on the conviction that only the proclamation of the Word of God and its free acceptance by the detainee can heal him in depth and make him rediscover faith in life.

The *Good Thief* should be presented to the prisoners, to the prostitutes, drunkards, dropouts and drug addicts, to the rebellious and rapists, as a friend to whom they can entrust themselves and to whom they can pray with faith to obtain the grace of such an encounter with mercy.

How the Contemplation on the Good Thief Will Restore the True Sense of the Good News of Mercy to the Church and the World

The whole Christian Revelation and Christian faith are summed up and contained in this truth: God is Love. And for the sinners that we are, this love becomes forgiveness and mercy.

Here is what the story of the Good Thief shows in a particular way:

- God's forgiveness is *unconditional* and requires no human "atonement," no "reparation." It requires no going back. It requires no "purgatory." To be sure, the Good Thief suffered horribly. He died in terrifying conditions. And no doubt his suffering and the way he died favored his conversion and faith; and no doubt, without this suffering and death, he would not have called upon the Savior's mercy. But his suffering and death in no way appear in the gospel as a punishment due to his sin, but only as the natural consequence of the evil he had committed, and these are caused only by the legal authority of men.

- God's forgiveness is totally and *freely-given*. It depends only on faith that opens man to grace. Trusting divine mercy is enough; it is given inasmuch as the sinner is willing to accept it.

- God's forgiveness is *immediate*. As soon as the sinner opens himself to the grace of forgiveness, the latter is granted immediately. As if the Saviour were waiting for this openness to rush with arms wide open and an open heart to grant his forgiveness. God is eager to be merciful and he waits, with an infinite and eternal patience, until he is able to forgive, because he totally respects the freedom of man. He waits with a consuming impatience, as the promptness of Jesus' answer shows, because God is passionate about man and his salvation.

- God's forgiveness is supremely *efficacious*. It brings about a radical re-creation, particularly manifested in the case of the Good Thief. In an instant, the latter moves from the state of the deepest servitude to sin to the loftiest height of holiness.

- God's forgiveness is *immeasurably beyond* what man can expect or even imagine. How could the Good Thief have imagined an access to "paradise" "on this very day," he, the first to enter it after "Paradise" had been closed by original sin to all the generations of men who followed? And the paradise that Jesus promises him is altogether different from the Kingdom he could have imagined: "With me," says Jesus! A divine intimacy!

A rediscovery of the devotion to the Good Thief, no doubt, will not make everyone perceive this whole teaching (and undoubtedly many other teachings) on the mercy of the Savior in a clear and explicit way. But it will help him grasp it in a vital and effective way that will inspire, encourage and stimulate him.

How Will the Good Thief Manage to be the Saint of Hope for All, Including the Great Sinners, the Wayward and the Marginalized

For the Good Thief to become the Saint of those people, he would first have to become the saint of the priests and apostles that God sends to them.

The holy priests of the Good Thief's "little way" are at our doors. They will be priests of mercy, priests with a childlike heart who, as Grignion de Montfort said, will come with poor means to perform wonders among the poor and the lowly.

The world and the Church need those priests with a merciful and fiery heart, announced by Grignion de Montfort. It seems to me that I already see them rise. These priests of mercy, formed by Mary's own devotion, will adopt Jesus as their model, he who forgave the Good Thief, the Samaritan woman and the adulteress. They will study in depth the episode of the holy thief to whom Jesus promises his paradise, they will meditate the parables of the Prodigal Son and the lost sheep. They will be merciful, leaning tenderly over the most distressed spiritually and all the rejected and wounded by life, the poorly loved, the forsaken and all the poor deprived of bread and light.

These merciful priests, these fathers of the prodigal sons and thieves of our world, will have a special love for the young generation in quest of truth and love. They will show unequivocally all the demands of the gospel, but will preach the almighty power of grace being displayed in weakness and will show themselves full of kindness for all the woeful. They will be priests with a childlike heart, raising apostles with fiery zeal among the lowly and the poor. They will be fathers with a merciful heart, without being paternalistic. They will be evangelizers with a fiery word, confessors and adorers.

They will renew the ministerial priesthood by the simplicity of their childlike heart. They will draw sinners who "will come near to them to hear them" and will sometimes shock some Pharisees, for they will be neither on the right nor on the left but in the center of the merciful Heart of Jesus.

Story of a Conversion

"The fact, reported by a woman religious of New York, was related in the periodical L'Univers. *In a suburb of New York, a young man of about twenty years lay dying, exhausted by a life of debauchery. As bad a son as he was a Christian, he had had only harsh words for his mother for a long time. She nonetheless begged him in tears to come back to God and to convert before his death. The young man responded with insults. Desperate, she ran to the neighboring church. The priest who was celebrating Mass was at the elevation. The mother fixed her eyes on the host and, taking the place of her son, repeated in faith the Good Thief's invocation: 'Lord, remember me when you come into your Kingdom!' For a few moments, she repeated her desolate plea while invoking the Good Thief, then, the Mass being ended; she went back to her son's bedside. She was greeted with these words she had not heard for years: 'Mother!' Then the dying man, pointing to the crucifix hanging on the wall: 'Mama, Christ looked at me. I saw him. I heard these words coming from him: 'Truly I tell you, today you will be with me in Paradise.' In haste, a priest was called. The young man made his confession in tears, received the last rites and died in peace."*

Poems for All the Thieves of the World

I live through nights...

I live through nights that could make me die of grief

That could break my heart and rend my soul
I live through nights that are like days
Too long to groan over and too dark for my veins.

I live through nights like a long corridor
Alone like a white pebble at the bottom of a big black lake
I live through nights as somber as a death
That pierces my soul and wounds and bites me

And I never run dry with bleeding tenderness
And I never stop harrowing my pain
But in this agony and in this offered mass
I beg you, my God, wrench out my heart.

I was awaiting you...

I was awaiting you, you see, as we await Love
I was laughing so often so as not to shed too many tears
I did not know the sweet peace of the soul
I was awaiting you by night, I was awaiting you by day

I stood watch by the window to catch a bit of sun
I was in the dark night and trembling with cold
I was twenty, no more, but already aged
I was awaiting you, you see, in the depth of my sleep

You came suddenly, crashing through my closed doors
To free my heart, to cleanse me in pure water
You came, my God, as Love alights
On the edge of the month of May, like a bouquet of roses.

A Love Song

In one blow, the spear pierced me, my Love

Here is my bleeding heart while I contemplate yours
And I hurt in your hands and my feet are nailed
And your night is my night and your cry is mine

Why do I weep as I watch your mother
Her sorrowful beauty is burning my eyes
And it is as if I were already breathing no more
Except the breath of the words you are whispering to her

The lash wounds me so much as it strikes your naked flesh
That I bleed from you as if I were your body
And here I am trembling on my knees at your feet
Seared with pain as I see you with bound arms

In one blow, the spear pierced you, you and me
See the blood and water and hear your last sigh
Love hurts so much as I feel your pain
That I would like to die crucified with you.

The Good Thief

There he was, lost, crying out in the dark night
There he was, more naked than a miserable earthworm
He had sought Love so much during his life
He had wandered so much in the depths of vast deserts

He had nothing, nothing more than a hurting child's heart
He had lost everything, his home and his life
He had nothing, nothing more than his darkened sins
He had sought Love so much while he lived

And then at the end, right close to his agony
He looked at the pierced Lamb of Tenderness
And entering into his Wounds, snuggling there like a child
He suddenly recognized his Beloved Father.

The Prodigal Son

When from the depths of mire I cry out my woe to you

You already rise, you rise, O my Father
And you watch for my step, you await my return
You are already exhausted wounded by love as you are

When all my sins sicken my heart
You already come to me with the waters of bliss
And you wish to cleanse me, you await my return
You are already sobbing, your heart bursting with love

And when I am coming over hill and dale
You rush towards me, both arms already opened wide
And you give me again the kiss of forgiveness
And you shed tears of joy and you leap with joy, O my Father.

The Guiltless

And he felt his heart, oppressed and torn

Nailed like a bird on the branch of the tree
Wounded like a lamb, silent and weeping
The snow of his wounds all melted into love

The thorns seared his satin smooth forehead
And the nails sank into his childlike flesh
And he cried out Father and the tears rolled
Like golden pearls in the morning sun

There he was, nailed, his whole body shedding blood
There he was, nailed, pierced all over
Taking upon himself, all our sins, our lusts
And feeling forsaken in the coming ages

But before breathing his last, he offered his final gift
So that each sinner might be forgiven
Through his wounds, he opened his Mother's pure heart
And placed all of us in the depths of his pain.

Hope

A child is born in me beyond my tears
On the threshold of my pain, at the cry of my wound
A child is born in me in the white dying winter
A child who will laugh after so many burns

There he is, I see him through the storms
The hoarfrost and the wind, the frost and the cold
There he is in my heart softly murmuring
That the nice days will come with their flowers and fruit

A child is singing in me, louder than my pain
Purer than my sin, smaller than my failings
A child is born in me, beyond the silence
And this is the child we call Hope.

In Spite of ...

In spite of the wound life has made on my heart
In spite of the ever running wound of my childhood
In spite of the throbbing pain on my back
In spite of the suffering that my friends each day nail on my soul

I will tell you the secret of my Joy
I will still speak to you of Happiness
I will cry to you Peace with the voice of my tears
I will declare that God is Love

In spite of my frailty, miseries and weakness
In spite of my falls, my pride, my senseless desires
In spite of the passing years that leave me unchanged
In spite of the shower of sins clinging to my bleeding flesh

I will always say yes to Life
I will speak to you of the wonders of the soul
I will cry out to you all the Beatitudes
I will declare that God is LOVE

In spite of bombs that are exploding
In spite of cities of steel polluted with sadness
In spite of the earth sobbing as it groans
In spite of the men my brothers fighting in their own house

I will proclaim the Good News
I will speak to you of the Holy Gospel
And beyond all human pain
The blood of the cross and the crown of thorns

I will write on your heart
With the blood of my life
That LOVE has come
And that it is named JESUS CHRIST.

Meditation on the Good Thief

"O blessed Thief! You received the grace of sharing the sufferings of my Savior. You were there beside Jesus on

> *the cross, the place where I myself would have wanted to be: the repentant and compassionate sinner. Your head leaned towards the divine Crucified One, mine is also leaning the same way. Most men loved the Christ of miracles and glory. But you loved him forsaken, in his pain and agony. Grant me who am also a thief, that at the hour of my death, I may receive pity and tenderness; and that the last beat of my poor heart may be, like yours, in a union of love with that of Christ Jesus dying for us. Amen."*

Félix-Antoine Savard, priest, 1977.

Come, all of you as well!

"Then Christ will say: 'Come, all of you as well! Come, all of you drunkards! Come, you weaklings! Come, you debauched!' And he will say: 'Vile beings, you are in the likeness of the beast and you bear his stamp. Come just the same, all of you!'

"And the wise will say, and the prudent will say: 'Lord why do you welcome them?' And he will say: 'If I welcome them, you, the wise, if I welcome them, you the prudent, it is because none of them ever thought he was worthy.' And he will open his arms to us, and we will fall at his feet, and then we will burst into tears, and we will understand everything, yes, we will understand everything."

Fyodr Dostoyevsky

Notes

Chapter 1

[1] All Scripture quotations are from the *New Revised Standard Version,* American edition, 1989.

2 Maria Winowska, *L'Icône du Christ miséricordieux,* Saint-Paul Ed. pp. 60-61.

[3] *Le Bon Larron, saint Dismas,* Spes Edition, Preface by Cardinal J.-G. Saliège.

[4] Latin translation of the Bible by St. Jerome, approved by the Council of Trent.

[5] Vittorio Messori, *Il a souffert sous Ponce Pilate, enquête historique sur la Passion et la mort de Jésus,* chap. 8, F.X. de Guibert Ed.

[6] *Op. cit.*

[7] A man sentenced to death has escaped... to paradise! (Luke 23:35, 43).

[8] Vittorio Messori, *Il a souffert sous Ponce Pilate.*

[9] Jean-Marc Varant, *Le Procès de Jésus.*

[10] Pilate did not understand that this was about a spiritual kingdom, and he did not attempt to understand ("What is the truth?"), he only understood that Jesus was innocent (and, no doubt, thought he was a visionary or a sectarian). The Good Thief, no doubt, did not understand any better, when he heard Jesus; then Jesus' words made their way into his mind. This text wishes to take the gospel data into account. Nevertheless, the presence of the criminals in the praetorium is deducted from our knowledge about the procedure of a trial in the Roman world of the time. Neither John's gospel nor the three synoptics give this information explicitly, but it is also true that the gospels are above all testimonies of faith and not a journalist's report of the time.

[11] In Mark, the crowd came to the praetorium to ask that a prisoner be graced, without thinking of Jesus' case. Pilate was the one who took advantage of this request to suggest that Jesus be graced and thus find his way out of an embarrassing situation, but his maneuver was upset by the chief priests, who suggested the name of Barabbas.

[12] A Roman citizen was beaten with whips made of poplar, ash, willow or vine branches; a soldier with a rigid club; a slave with the *flagellum*. The term *aule* (courtyard) in Mark indicates that the scourging of Jesus (and no doubt that of the criminals as well) took place inside the royal palace.

[13] *Causa poenae* in Roman law, "the motive of the sentence." Suetonius, *The life of Caligula;* Eusebius, *Ecclesiastical History* 5, 1-4.

[14] Recent archeological discoveries confirm the use of the three languages as noted by John.

[15] *Letter 101* from Seneca to Lucillium.

[16] Cicero in *Verrem II* (5, 168-169).

[17] *Golgotha* in Hebrew, *Gulgaltha* in Aramaic, *Calvarum* in Latin. Archeologists set this place inside the basilica of the Holy Sepulcher.

[18] The right heel was placed over the left heel, and a nail was driven through the feet in this trajectory. This nail served as a support for the crucified victims to prevent them from being strangled. This is evident on the shroud of Turin, the authenticity of which was again confirmed by recent studies.

[19] Lagrange, *L'Évangile selon saint Luc*, quoted by Dom Dubois in *Dictionnaire du catholicisme*, pp. 589-591.

[20] Recent medical experiments corroborate a certain number of ancient extra-biblical sources that make crucified individuals talk.

[21] The Evil Thief addresses Jesus as "Messiah" (v. 39); the Good Thief recognizes him as "king" (v. 42). These are the two titles – religious and political – around which Jesus' whole trial revolved, first before the Jews, then before Pilate (*Bible of Jerusalem*, 1954, Luke 23:35, note d).

[22] See vol. 3, pp. 637-638, Editions of 1888.

Chapter 2

[23] *Commentariorum in Mat.* 2.

[24] *Commentaires sur l'Épître aux Romains* 3:27-28.

[25] *De Coena Domini.*

[26] *Epist.* 58,1.

[27] *Epist, Ad Jubaianom* 73, 22.

[28] *De Coena Domini*, 4. *Epist.* 58:1.

[29] Allegorical exegesis of *In Mattheum* 33,5.

[30] *Expositio Evangelii secundum Lucam* 10, 121.

[31] *Sermon pour la Parascève.*

[32] *Catec.* XIII.

[33] *Cat. de 40 mart.*

[34] *Homelia de chananaea.*

[35] *In Gen. S.* VII.

[36] *In Gen. S.* VII.

[37] *In Gen. S.* VII.

[38] *In Gen. S.* VII.

[39] *De coeco nato.*

[40] *De coeco nato.*

[41] *Sermo in Parasc.*

[42] *In Ps. 137.*

[43] *In Gen. S.* VII.

[44] *In Gen. S.* VII.

[45] *In Gen. S.* VII.

[46] *In Gen. S.* VII.

[47] *Epist.*XIII to the Paulin.

[48] *Sermo* XLV.

[49] *Sermo* 44, 155.

[50] *Enarratio in Ps.* 35:15; 34:14.

[51] *Enarratio in Ps.* 35:15; 34:14.

[52] *De diversis questionibus* 83.

[53] *De Baptismo contra donatistas.*

[54] *De anima et ejus orig.*

[55] *In Joan.*

[56] 75,2, P. 314.

[57] *Sermo XI de Pass. Domini.*

[58] *Sermo II de Pass.*

[59] In *Métamorphose du Bon Larron, devenu apôtre*, from Fr. Théophile Raynaud, S.J.

[60] *Bibl. Max.* T. 13.

[61] *Commentaires de Luc* 23.

Chapter 3

[62] Maurice Zundel, quoted in *L'Humble Présence*, Tricorne Ed., p. 108.

[63] *Agenda* 1948, 21, 23 and 24 January.

[64] *Idées modernes, réponses chrétiennes*, Téqui, p. 169.

[65] Bernard Bro, *La Gloire et le Mendiant*, Cerf Ed., p. 199.

[66] "Lettre pour le 3e centenaire de saint Paul de la Croix," *Doc. Cath.,* n° 2107, p. 9.

[67] Jacques Maritain,*The Peasant of the Garonne*, Wolt Rinehart and Winston, 1968, pp. 243-244.

[68] Le Visage intérieur, Stock, p. 280.

Chapter 4

[69] Origen inaugurating the allegorical exegesis of Lk 23:42-43.

[70] Jean-Miguel Garrigues, *Dieu sans idée du mal*, Desclée, p. 181.

[71] *Entretiens sur la grâce*, DDB, pp. 102-103.

[72] *Raïssa's Journal*, presented by Jacques Maritain, Magi Books, p. 393.

[73] "Everything in man that refuses to die is unworthy of life." Gustave Thibon, in *L'Échelle de Jacob*

[74] "The more I think of this, the more I find that death, by the great intuition and invasion of the All New, is a liberation and a relief ... It would be so stifling to feel irremediably confined to the superficial and experimental face of the cosmos" (Teilhard de Chardin).

[75] Quoted by F.-X. Durrwell, in *Christ,Hunankind and Death,* Mediaspaul, 59..

[76] Saint Paul Ed., p. 13.

Chapter 5

[77] Interview with Cardinal Danneels on Thérèse of Lisieux in *30 jours*, n° 57, May 1997.

[78] H. U. von Balthasar, *Élisabeth de la Trinité et sa mission spirituelle*, Seuil, p. 130.

[79] F.-X. Durrwell, *In the Redeeming Christ*, Sheed and Ward, p. 176.

[80] Cardinal Jean Daniélou, *Myth and Mystery*, Hawthorne Books, p. 51.

[81] *Reconciliation and Penance*, n° 13.

[82] Desclée de Brouwer, p. 26.

[83] Osservatore romano, French edition, November 1988.

[84] Canonization is the official registration by the Church in the catalog of saints. Jesus' declaration is not a "canonization" in the strict sense of the word. It expresses no less, it says much more. At such a moment, the Son of God spoke only of what was close to his heart and appeared extremely important to him.

[85] Albert Bessières, S.J., *Le Bon Larron*, Spes.

[86] Of whom the most recent one could be Jacques Fesch, this young man sentenced to death and executed on 1st October 1957, after a dazzling conversion during his detention in the La Santé prison. Cf. *Dans cinq heures, je verrai Jésus! Journal de prison* (*In five hours, I will see Jesus!* Prison diary) by Jacques Fesch, Fayard. In fact, Cardinal Jean-Marie Lustiger has just announced the opening of the preliminary investigation in view of his possible beatification.

Chapter 6

[87] John Paul II, *On the Mercy of God*, n° 9.

[88] Frederick William Faber, *The Foot of the Cross*, p. 252.

[89] "Marie, Mère du Christ et des chrétiens," *Foi Vivante*.

[90] The Liturgical Press, Collegeville, pp. 24 and 26.

[91] John Paul II, *On the Mercy of God*, n° 9.

[92] W. Sténissen, *La nuit comme le jour illumine*, du Moustier Ed., p. 85.

[93] Quoted in *La Faibless transfigurée*, Le Renouveau Ed., p. 31.

[94] *Un poète regarde la croix*, pp. 114-115.

Chapter 7

[95] Words from Sister Geneviève – Céline, Thérèse's sister – quoted by Fr. Molinié in *Le Courage d'avoir peur* (The courage to fear).

[96] This is about the commentary of 20 May 1993 by Dom Claude Richard, abbot of the Cistercian monastery of Our Lady of Timadeuc.

[97] *Autobiography of St. Thérèse of Lisieux*, trans. Ronald Knox (New York: P.J.Kennedy & Sons, 1958) p. 312.

[98] *Novissima Verba*, 11 July 1897.

[99] *Conseils et souvenirs*, Central Office at Lisieux, 1952, p. 41.

[100] This is a story drawn from *Vies des Pères des déserts d'Orient*. A woman named Paesia, a public sinner, was so totally converted one day that she was ready to atone for her sins by doing penance for a long time. However, God recalled her to himself that very night, and the hermit who was bringing her to a monastery saw a beam of light coming down from heaven on Paesia and being used as a road by several angels who were carrying her soul to heaven. At the same time, he heard a miraculous voice telling him: "Her penance of one hour was more agreeable to God than the one that others make for a long time, because they do not do it with as much fervor as she did" (cf. *Histoire d'une âme*, pp. 324-326).

[101] To Sister Marie du Sacré-Coeur, 8 September 1896.

[102] Letter 124 to Céline, 20 October 1890.

[103] Letter to Sister Agnès, 3 September 1890.

[104] Letter 224 to Fr. Bellière, 25 April 1897.

[105] See also *Histoire d'une âme*, p. 205.

[106] Letter 197 to Sister Marie du Sacré-Coeur, 17 September 1896, commonly called *The Charter of Little Souls*.

[107] *Conseils et souvenirs*.

[108] Letter to Fr. Roulland.

[109] *Oeuvres complètes*, p. 144.

[110] 9 June 1895.

[111] Letter 197 of 17 September 1896.

[112] Excerpt from his excellent little book *Thérèse, dis-nous ton secret!* (Thérèse, tell us your secret), Le Sarment-Fayard.

Chapter 8

[113] In *Ps IV*.

[114] Peter of Natalibus was the first compiler to mention the Good Thief in his *Catalog III* published in 1372. He calls him *Dismas*. Baronius also registered him in the Roman martyrology but without attributing a name to him and by giving him the title of confessor, on 25 March, commonly accepted in the past as the date of Christ's death (cf. "Saint Dismas," *Dictionnaire du catholicisme*, vol. 3, col. 886, Letouzey and Ané, by Dom Jacques Dubois). Recent studies move the date of Christ's death to 14 or 15 *nisan*, likely 7 April of the year 30 of our era.

[115] Norm 18 accompanying the apostolic constitution *Indulgentiarum doctrina*, by Paul VI.

[116] *La Grâce et nous, chrétiens*, Fayard, p. 111.

CPSIA information can be obtained
at www.ICGtesting.com
Printed in the USA
BVHW071452270220
573515BV00002B/236